Candle Crafting Made Easy: Ultimate Guide

Nadir .E Carty

All rights reserved. Copyright © 2023 Nadir .E Carty

<u>Funny helpful tips:</u>

Your spirit is a flame; keep it burning brightly, illuminating your path.

Limit sugar intake; excessive sugar can lead to weight gain, energy crashes, and long-term health issues.

Candle Crafting Made Easy: Ultimate Guide : Discover The Secrets To Creating Beautiful Candles From Home: The Complete Step-By-Step Guide to Candle Making

Life advices:

Seek shared values; they offer a strong foundation.

Stay connected to nature; it grounds and rejuvenates the spirit.

Introduction

Welcome to this guide. In this comprehensive guide, you'll discover the fascinating history of candle making, the significance of beeswax, and step-by-step instructions to create beautiful beeswax candles from the comfort of your home.

The journey begins with exploring the history of candle making, from its early forms to its evolution through the centuries. Beeswax candles have a unique place in this history, influenced by factors like the surging whaling industry and innovations in colonial times. Discover the importance of candles in colonial America and how their legacy impacts the candles we use today.

You'll delve into the process of harvesting and processing beeswax cappings, a critical step in creating beeswax candles. Learn how to render and purify beeswax, preparing it for candle making. Discover the materials required and the techniques to melt and store beeswax cappings effectively.

As you progress, you'll find detailed instructions for making beeswax candles at home. Learn valuable tips like keeping an eye on melting beeswax, choosing the right ingredients, and setting up your workspace. Explore different methods of candle making, from using heat-proof pour cups to lubricating molds and selecting the perfect wick.

Experiment with various recipes to add fun and creativity to your candle making journey. Discover how to make scented candles using essential oils, create colored candles, and even paint your homemade candles using different techniques. From lavender candles to coffee-scented delights, the guide provides step-by-step instructions for each unique recipe.

While on your candle-making adventure, you'll encounter common mistakes and how to avoid them. From preventing tunneling to addressing poor fragrance and avoiding cracks in your candles, you'll gain insights into troubleshooting and improving your candle-making skills.

Whether you're a complete beginner or have some experience, this guide equips you with the knowledge and techniques needed to create exquisite beeswax candles. From understanding the history to mastering the art of candle making, you're on your way to crafting beautiful and fragrant candles that will light up your space and add a touch of creativity to your life. Get ready to embark on a journey of creativity and craftsmanship with beeswax candle making!

Contents

Chapter I: The History of Candle Making The early candles 1
    Earliest types of portable illumination 1
    Early candles were used on religious occasions 2
    Candle making in the Middle Ages 2
    Candle making art has remained more or less similar 2
    Influence of America's surging whaling industry 3
The introduction of beeswax candles 3
Candles in the colonial times 5
    Why were candles important in colonial times? 5
    Evolution in candle making process during Colonialtimes 5
    Today's candles are impacted by innovations in thecolonial times 7
Advances in candle making in the 19th century 8
    Candles were popular in Victorian era 8
    The 19th century - defining time period for candlemaking 8
    Use of paraffin wax for the first time 9
    Development of machine for candle making 9
The candle as we know today 10
    Many other uses of candles 11
    Today's candles 12
Chapter II: Harvesting and ProcessingBeeswax Cappings 14
Applications of beeswax 16
Materials required 19
Rendering beeswax from the honeycomb 19
Purification of the beeswax 21
Melting the beeswax cappings 24

Storing your beeswax cappings 27
Chapter III: Making Candles Out of Beeswax at Home 29
Things to remember while making beeswax candles 33
    Keep an eye on a beeswax while it melts 33
    Reduce melting point by mixing palm or coconut oil 33
    Choose beeswax granules instead of blocks 34
    Handling cracking problems 35
    Ingredients required 35
    What should you know prior to getting started? 35
Where can you find all the ingredients required for making beeswax candles? 36
    Basic ingredients to make beeswax candles at home 36
Make Sure You Have the Right Equipment for Making Beeswax Candles at Home . 38
    Create a distinct workspace 38
    Look out for a pouring pot 39
    Make your own double boiler 40
    Purchasing wax for candle making 40
    Get a thermometer 41
    Candlewick 41
    Recycling or repurposing jar 42
    Scents 42
    Dyes 42
Instructions for making your very own beeswax candles 43
    Materials needed 43
    Instructions 44
Chapter IV: The Different Methods of Making Candles 47
    Heat proof pour cup 47
    Lubricating the mold 47
    Straight wicks 47

- The different types of wicks 48
- How to choose the right wick for your candle? 51
  - Add a little fragrance by making your beeswax candles with essential oils 53
- Making colored beeswax candles 54
  - Painting your homemade candles: Materials and techniques 57
  - Conventional painting 58
  - Materials needed 58
- Using paper transfer technique 59
  - Materials needed 59
  - Making streaked candles 60
  - Materials needed 60
- A few ideas on decorating your homemade beeswax candles 61
- Chapter V: Fun Recipes to Try Out While Making Candles at Home 64
- Recipe for lavender candles 64
  - Supplies or ingredients required 65
  - Steps for making these candles 65
- Recipe for homemade crayon candles 66
  - Steps for preparing crayon candles at home 67
- Fun recipe for making beeswax candles with forest scents (essential oils) 68
  - Ingredients or supplies for forest scented beeswax candles 69
  - Ingredients for making woods scented beeswax candle 69
- Fun recipe for making DIY coffee candles 70
  - Preparations or ingredients 70
  - How to get started? 71
  - Wax making procedure 71
  - Time for adding the coffee 71
  - Make your DIY candle now 72
  - Begin the pouring process 72

Your coffee candle is ready now 72
Fun recipe for making DIY Aromatherapy beeswaxcandles 73
    How to select the right quality of essential oils for yourhomemade aromatherapy candles? 73
    Ingredients or supplies needed 74
    Steps for aromatherapy homemade candles are asfollows 74
Scented holiday candles with multiple layers 76
    Ingredients or supplies required 76
Recipe for DIY French Vanilla candle with coffeebeans 77
    Supplies or ingredients needed 77
    Steps 78
Recipe for homemade Eucalyptus candles withessential oils 79
    Supplies or ingredients required 79
    Are you ready to start? 80
Fun recipe for making votive candles at home 81
    Supplies or ingredients required 81
    Steps 82
Chapter VI: Common Mistakes to Avoid WhileMaking Candles at Home 85
Candle tunneling 86
What to do when your candle has a poorfragrance? 87
Does your candle smoke as it burns? 89
What to do when the candle does not come out ofthe molds? 90
How to avoid cracks in your candles? 91
Does your finished candle show signs of bubblesand pitting? 92

Chapter I: The History of Candle Making

The early candles

While candles have been used to illuminate celebrations and for lighting for over 5,000 years, not much is written about how they originated.

Some experts have mentioned that the ancient Egyptians were the first to develop candles in the world. They used torches (also known as rush lights) that were made by the reeds' cores soaked into melted animal fat. Yet, these rush lights did not have a wick like a real candle.

Earliest types of portable illumination

Candles are an initial type of portable illumination; these have served important functions for mankind throughout the history. The invention of candles is seen among all societies. Factually, the use of candles has been chronicled just like objects.

Historians feel that the original candles could have been discovered by primitive humankind. They believe that these people dried branches and dipped them into animal fat that produced a reliable and a slow-burning source of light.

Ancient Egyptian relics depict that philosophers and writers used candles as they worked for long hours even after the sunset. Another interesting point is that people from the Crete Island used dish-shaped candles around 3,000 B.C.

Early candles were used on religious occasions

It is believed that the early candles were used on various religious occasions. For instance, the Bible makes a number of references on the use of early candles. The story of the famous King Solomon is a notable one among all these. The king built the Temple and subsequently is believed to have used 10 candle-sticks for lighting the temple's north as well as the south ends.

Candle making in the Middle Ages

Candle making was an extremely popular occupation during the Middle Ages. It can be ascertained from the creation of innumerable guilds of candle makers all through Europe. Subsequently, the candles were used for the purpose of timekeeping. When auctions were conducted, the limitation on the bidding time was imposed by insertion of a pin into one of the candles. The wax was then allowed to melt until the drop of the pin. Thus, the time period for bidding was concluded.

Candle making art has remained more or less similar

Surprisingly, the candle making art has remained more or less similar to the initial production procedures; the materials comprising the candles, nonetheless, have undergone changes. Candle wicks were first made of rushes or reeds. Subsequently, a number of natural fibers were used for candle making.

Frenchman Jean-Jacques Cambaraceres came up with a key refinement in the field of wick technology. He made use of the plaited wick, which burned in a more even manner as compared to the earlier plaited wicks. In fact, a majority of wick candles are made from plaited or twisted cotton even today.

While vegetable or animal fats were used for making the first candles, bee wax was more common. It was widely used with the progress in candle making technology. The objective for this is its pleasant scent as well as no mess, both of which were usually present when the animal fats melted in the earlier times.

Influence of America's surging whaling industry

America's whaling industry saw a huge surge post the Revolutionary War era. The key reason for the popularity of the then spermaceti candle was because it lacked acidic scent. It retained its texture even in high summer temperatures. These candles also burned in an even manner.

The candle makers separated the animal fats as candle technology advanced. The separation left behind desirable fatty acids with a solid texture like stearine, which was odorless and had a brighter light. Paraffin was sourced later on from petroleum, which gained immense popularity during the 1860s.

The introduction of beeswax candles

It is sad that, while a majority of candles today do not contain lead wicks that are toxic in nature, at times the ones that you buy from stores may have junk in them. This junk could be in the form of paraffin and artificial odor. To put it simply, you would not desire to feel them in the air of the home. Candles made from beeswax are extremely popular; they offer a host of merits. Read on to discover some of the top advantages of beeswax candles.

Great smell

Beeswax candles smell good. Their scent is naturally due to the honeycomb's floral nectar; and, it is real honey.

These candles are non-toxic, safe and environmentally friendly

These candles burn in a clean way. The candles emit very little smoke if trimmed well since they are not based on oil. When you buy 100 percent beeswax candles, they are naturally biodegradable. Therefore, they do not undergo any kind of chemical processing.

Sourced from the bees, natural and free from chemicals

They are the most ancient candles known to humans. You need to understand, however, that certain candles that are sold under the label of beeswax could be made of paraffin. These so-called beeswax candles can contain only five percent beeswax. The trick is that you need to look for beeswax candles that are 100 percent pure.

Melting point of beeswax candles is high

The melting point is very high. Its massive burn time is two to five times higher than other candles; similarly, these candles drip very little. It is a feature that commensurates for their high costs.

Beeswax candles are known to be hypo-allergic in nature

These candles, for the above-mentioned reasons, benefit all those people who suffer from conditions such as asthma, sensitivities, and allergies.

They can burn brighter and stronger

Beeswax candles can emit bright light and are a great gift from nature. Their light spectrum is the same as that of the sun.

Candles in the colonial times

Did you ever wonder how people in colonial times made candles? Though the techniques used for their candle making were drastically different in comparison to the present procedures, people in the colonial times can be attributed to much significant advancement in the techniques for candle making. These people were highly resourceful and frugal. They relied upon candles to a large extent. This lead them to come up with certain techniques in candle making. These practices are still followed.

Why were candles important in colonial times?

A majority of people today find the presence of candles enjoyable. Candles are helpful in creating a soothing or romantic ambiance while adding an element of warmth and color to a room. They fill the air of your house with fragrant scents. Although many people have a fondness for candles, you need to remember that they are not an absolute necessity anymore. They can be replaced by other light sources (such as lamps).

Evening hours used to be precious time. People had to complete a lot of daily work. Household work could not be finished in the dark and in the long evenings, women in the colonial times depended on candles as the key source of light for their homes.

Evolution in candle making process during Colonial times

Tallow
People in Colonial times created candles by rendering animal fats, just like the generations that came before them. This process rendered a substance known as tallow. It is possible to melt and dip tallow in order to create fat and taper candles. On the other

hand, the texture of the tapers was much softer as compared to today's candles. In fact, they smelled bad and dripped excessively. Candles made from tallow burned with a dim light due to their excessive softness. They also did not last for a long time.

Yet, procuring tallow was easier and it was possible to make candles in bigger batches at the house. Women came together to make an adequate quantity of tallow candles when the temperature dropped during the fall each year. The tallow candles were made to last through the long and cold winter months.

Bayberry Wax

A new type of wax was also extracted from bayberries. The wax made from bayberry was hard. It did not run or drip like tallow and it had a good smell. It was seen as a great alternative since bayberries could be procured easily. The real problem was, in spite of this, that it was a time-consuming process. The maker had to use several pounds of these berries to create only a single candle. Use of bayberry candle just did not appear to be practical.

Beeswax

Colonial people with some extra money opted for rolled beeswax candles. These candles have a nice scent and last for a longer duration; although, these candles were costly.

Spermaceti/Whale Oil Wax

Whale oil was a bi-product sourced from the then-surging whale industry. This oil was available to colonial people by the end of the eighteenth century. The whale oil produced a substance known as spermaceti wax which created harder candles.

Before those times, the candles had to be dipped. This made each candle slightly different from one another. The candles created became uniform once candle molds were invented and a harder wax was used. People during the colonial times made candle molds from wood in order to utilize spermaceti wax for the production of candles. Thereafter, they went ahead and created the first standard candles.

Families that did not have the financial ability to afford the purchase of huge volumes of spermaceti wax could buy them in smaller quantity. It was mixed with tallow to create harder candles, which could be stored quite easily.

Those whose access to the wax was immediate, like people employed in the whaling industry, enjoyed the liberty to make candles at any time of the year. They did not have to worry about the weather constantly changing, for they got to store candles safely.

Today's candles are impacted by innovations in the colonial times

It is possible for you to buy bayberry candles today and find out how they burn in a clean way. The most crucial innovation in the colonial times, however, has been the use of a candle mold to create the standard candle. Candles with uniform shape and size are a common phenomenon these days. It has been possible due to the increased popularity and demand of candle molds for today's candle makers.

Advances in candle making in the 19th century

Today, the candle making industry has become a highly profitable and competitive industry. Hence, it is imperative to study the past. It is the finest way to introduce innovative and new paths forward. After all, there is something new for all to learn while moving ahead as we look back.

Candles were popular in Victorian era

All upper-class households during the Victorian era were known to use candles along with their accessories. Affluent people who took pride in their elegant houses used candelabra positioned right in front of their tall and long glass mirrors. This period witnessed the use of a variety of candles. While some of them featured shades, other candles were tasseled or frilled. There were even others that were made of paper or were plain.

The 19th century - defining time period for candle making

The nineteenth century was a defining era for candle making. Patented machines for making candles were introduced for the first time. It was a major breakthrough that enabled people from all segments of society to start purchasing candles. Chemist Michael Eugene Chevreul discovered that animal fat or tallow consisted of different fatty acids during the same time period.

He also identified a fatty acid called stearic acid or stearine. Chevreul, along with Chemist Joseph Gay Lussac, procured a patent from crude stearic for candle making in 1825. It was a big development, for there was a drastic improvement in the candle quality. Prior to this time, wicks were just made by twisting cotton strands; they burned poorly as a result. Plus, these candles required constant maintenance.

Use of paraffin wax for the first time

It was somewhere in the nineteenth century (in the 1850s) when the use of paraffin wax was made for the first time. This first appeared in a candle within the United Kingdom. Chemists by then had learned means of separating the wax material from petroleum; then, they refined the substance further.
The development resulted in paraffin getting produced on a commercial scale. Paraffin was odorless, burning bright and clean. The product was also mixed with stearic acid that made the wax even harder. It led to the creation of a cheaper but superior candle, as compared to other types of candles.

Paraffin has a bluish-white hue and became a blessing to the candle making industry due to its above-mentioned features. Its low melting point was the only demerit from which it suffered. However, that was soon taken care of by including stearic acid. It was already widely available and quite easily accessible.

Development of machine for candle making

Joseph Morgan, a renowned inventor, helped in the further advancement of the present-day candle industry. In 1834, he introduced the machine which enabled the production of continuously molded candles. It was made possible by making use of a special cylinder which featured a movable piston. This ejected the candles when they solidified. Candles became extremely affordable for the general masses as mechanized production was introduced.

Today, candle lovers enjoy a great variety of candles in the candle market that are produced from different kinds of waxes. Some of them are: bee wax, vegetable wax, gel wax (the newest variety) and paraffin. These candles are available in a great variety of fragrances, designs, shapes, and colors. While candles are not the only source of light anymore, they can add to the ambiance of your homes through their sweet fragrances and serve as excellent items for decoration.

The candle as we know today

Lamps and candles were widely used in houses for illumination before electric lights were invented. Candles were more widely used in Northern Europe until the twentieth century. In fact, they are used extensively, even today in localities without electricity. On the other hand, the use of oil lamps was predominant in the Mediterranean and Southern Europe..

Today, candles are used in many developed nations primarily for their scent and aesthetic value. They create a romantic, warm or soft ambiance. They are also used for emergency lighting during power failures, as well as for ritual or religious purposes.

Many other uses of candles

Candles were earlier used to notify the time since a candle's burning time is measurable and consistent. Such candles were specifically designed for measuring time, whereas hours were usually marked distinctly along its wax. In China, the Song Dynasty was known to use candle clocks.

As the eighteenth century arrived, candle clocks were specially created with weights put on both their sides. The weights dropped when the candle melted. These weights naturally made a noise when they fell off into a bowl.

A crucial role is played by candles in several winter vacations. After all, candlelight not only looks mesmerizing and lovely, but it also has a special significance attached to it for these special occasions.

During the Christmas season, a candle is burned by some people up to a certain amount to indicate a day, as per the mark made on that candle. Such a type of candle used for measuring a day is referred to as the Advent candle.

The Jews celebrate a holiday they refer to as "The Festival of Lights" or Hanukkah. They lit a candle in the night on a candelabrum or the menorah which can hold nine candles. While eight candles out of these signify Hanukkah's eight nights, ninth candle is known as the "shamash." It is used for lighting the other candles.

People use lights and candles in so many different ways throughout Christmas. Some use them to depict the famous star over the city of Bethlehem, while others light a candle on all of the four weeks during Advent. Advent is used to denote four weeks before the arrival of Christmas.

Today's candles

As time passed, different types of materials were being used for candle making. Most candles today are created from paraffin. This generates less smoke so that candles burn cleaner. As discussed earlier, paraffin is a waxy byproduct sourced from petroleum refining. The substance was distilled for the first time in 1830. It has revolutionized the process of candle making due to its host of benefits such as being odorless, clean burning and economical.

A majority of the candle makers today use contemporary and sophisticated candle manufacturing equipment, such as molds, so that they can do mass production of the candles. The candle manufacturers are traditionally referred to as "chandlers". The basic candle production technique constitutes of melting the paraffin or the solidified material; then, this substance is poured into a special mold until the material cools.

There are some artists who still like to make candles in the time-tested old-fashioned manner by dipping the wick into hot paraffin or other waxy substances, such as beeswax. After repeated dipping, a basic candle can be created by these artists.

Many candle artisans frequently include scents and dyes so that they can come up with a large range of customized candles. These candles, in turn, smell good and look lovely while they burn. There are several people today who purchase homemade custom candles as precious items of art or as decorations for their homes.

Chapter II: Harvesting and Processing Beeswax Cappings

What is beeswax?

Beeswax is an essential ingredient for the process of candle making. If beeswax did not exist, then there would definitely never be beeswax candles. You would most probably not be reading about beeswax candle making. The wonderful thing about beeswax is that it emits its own fragrance of sweet honey. Quite a good number of people do not know anything about beeswax. This section aims to enlighten people regarding this.

In simple words, beeswax is an organic material which is produced by the female worker honey bees through the glands found under their belly. This secretion is commonly called beeswax scale. The average width of the scale is about three millimeters and it usually is irregular in shape. Each gram of beeswax needs about two thousand of these beeswax scales to be made. So, the amount of wax needed for an average beeswax candle comes from about a million beeswax scales. If the scales are smaller than average which does happen at times, then this number can be significantly larger.

Intrinsically, beeswax is white in color or see through; this is based on how thick the scales are. The thickness of the scales produced by the bees depends on their age. Bees that are young or old produce slim scales, whereas the middle-aged ones produce dense scales.

For the secretion of wax to take place, the temperature of the hive needs to be approximately ninety-seven degrees Fahrenheit. It is observed that the rate of wax production witnesses a rise during the months of April to June, due to the queens endeavor to repopulate the colony and consequent surplus flow of nectar. This happens to be the precursor to honey. Most experts believe that, due to the massive deluge of honey being produced, bees step up their scale production to make more room to store the honey made.

There are four species of honey bees out there in the world; however, most of the man-made products utilize the beeswax produced by a species called Apis mellifera. The remaining species of bees produce meager amounts of beeswax, including honey, and are difficult to work with; hence, they are not preferred.

A surprising fact of which most people are unaware is that bees need to consume honey to make the scales. Research has indicated variations in the amount of honey consumed; however, on an average, about eight to ten portions of honey goes into producing a single unit of beeswax. Bees which are producing wax do not engage in any other work apart from the secreting. Once the wax is secreted, it is the worker bees' responsibility to amass them into honeycomb.

The shape of the honeycomb cells is believed to be hexagonal because of the rigidity it offers in comparison to other shapes. These honeycombs are used to hoard both the honey and the larvae of the bees.

Although beeswax candles come in multitudes of colors, the actual color of the beeswax varies on its origin and hygiene. Beeswax from infected hives are usually brownish in color and are unfit for use. It has been observed that beeswax with brownish tinge often have chemicals in them owing to their origins, and so such beeswax is sold cheap. The premium quality beeswax is either cream or white in color. However, this color is not natural and results from chemical refining. Beeswax is naturally gold in color due to the nectar and pollen stored in them.

Once the comb is full of honey, it is covered with white beeswax upon ripening. Most beeswax candle makers return the honeycomb to the bees once they are done with it. The candles are exclusively made from the new hygienic beeswax taken from the outermost honeycomb cells, post the extraction of honey.

In terms of chemical elements, beeswax comprises of at least two hundred and eighty-four constituents. On the contrary, pure beeswax comprises of only oxygen, hydrogen and carbon. It has been found that, the sweet fragrance of honey originates from only about fifty of the constituents found in beeswax. The beeswax is not directly used; it is cleaned and refined for hygiene reasons.

Applications of beeswax

The uses of beeswax have been known from a long time as cited by the various annals and folklore. This has been noted from the legend of the Icarus who flew in close proximity to the sun utilizing wings made out of beeswax to the broth invented by Pilyn, which supposedly cured dysentery. The bottom line is that beeswax has been in use long before now. It has been found that certain cultures utilized beeswax as a currency as well. When the Romans overthrew Corsicans, they are said to have levied a tax of ten thousand pounds of beeswax. French farmers were supposed to pay a yearly tax of two pounds of beeswax in the 1300s. It is a testimony to the fact that beeswax was extremely precious back in the olden days. Making this argument stronger is the fact that the Catholic Church in Rome made a rule that only beeswax candles need to be used in prayers and other services. Surprisingly, beeswax is still used for many purposes currently. Some of them are as follows:

As a lubricant

Most people do not realize that beeswax is an excellent lubricant. It is especially used to oil old furniture joints. In addition to furniture joints, it can also be used to smoothen the movement of windows and doors.

As a mustache cream

A good number of mustache creams use beeswax as the key ingredient. By applying these creams, men can harden their mustaches and shape it as they wish. It can easily be made at home, provided that some beeswax is accessible. All it requires is just melting of about eight ounces of beeswax in a Bain Marie (a type of double boiler). Then, mix it with four ounces of petroleum jelly. It is ready to be used after the mixture cools.

To preserve the metal articles

Moisture in the air is responsible for the tarnishing of bronze articles. In order to keep the moisture from making contact with the surface of the bronze, a solution of beeswax and turpentine may be applied on the surface. This sticks to the surface as a protective coat. Applying molten beeswax on the surface of copper is found to protect it. Also, most iron articles are coated with beeswax to prevent rusting.

Lubing for jewelry making

Most people do not know that jewelers often use beeswax for lubing purposes, such as when carving intricate strands from precious metals like gold and silver.

As a glazing agent

A lot of cheese makers utilize beeswax for glazing purposes in order to protect the cheese from contamination. Although plastic was used for some time, it was found that it imparted an unpleasant zest to the cheese. It is not used any longer for this reason.

As a wood conditioner

An excellent wooden conditioner can be prepared by heating a mixture comprising of one part of edible inorganic oil and five parts beeswax. The ratios of beeswax and oil may be varied to get a thicker paste if needed. It is commonly used to condition wooden articles like bowls and boards.

To tackle oil spills

Most people are unaware that NASA uses a blend of beeswax and some enzymes to eliminate cases of oil spillage. The beeswax absorbs all of the oil, while the enzymes decompose it. This can be utilized to clear oil spills in oceans as well.

To make sweets

Fruit gums, jelly beans, and other sweets, such as toffees, are fabricated from beeswax. Beeswax gives these sweets their texture and holds all the flavor without allowing it to get debilitated.

For protection of leather

People take great care to ensure that their expensive leather does not come in contact with water. One of the best ways to protect leather from water is to apply a smelted mixture of beeswax with tallow and neat's-foot oil all in equivalent ratios.

To polish Granite

Molten beeswax is the best polish for granite counters, for it cleans it up like magic. It is spread evenly on the granite surface and intended to be used as a polish. Then, after some time, it is wiped with a smooth piece of cloth. The surface will get its sheen back like it is brand new.

Materials required

We are going to discuss the process of rendering beeswax. It is a single stage purification procedure; there is no need to filter again and again. Most of the processes for rendering beeswax require melting the beeswax more than once; this makes it cumbersome and time consuming. Most of the other rendering methods are slight variations of the crude method of rendering beeswax. We are going to discuss the process of rendering, which is way more efficient than the crude methods or its variants. In this section, we shall list all the items required to render beeswax efficiently.

The list of items needed to render beeswax are:

- A sizable old container which can withstand heat, since traces of wax are likely to stick on to it after the rendering. It is recommended to use some old, disposable container.
- A good quality cheesecloth which has a high thread count. The higher the thread count, the more suited it is to this procedure.
- Some tight cloth clips or pegs, preferable made out of plastic, so that they do not get heated up easily.
- Amassed beeswax which is as clean as possible
- Long metal tongs with sufficient width for gripping them tightly.

Rendering beeswax from the honeycomb

The procedure of rendering beeswax from honeycomb takes about forty to forty-five minutes to complete. This excludes the time for it to cool off. The procedure we are about to discuss is a single stage refinement procedure.

One of the crude methods of rendering beeswax involves melting it directly in a container of water after which the impurities are removed through a strainer. This is followed by pouring it through a filter paper to get rid of all the micro impurities. The filtering process is repeated many times till the beeswax is refined to the maximum extent possible. This process is both cumbersome and time-consuming. We are going to discuss a far simpler and more efficient method to render beeswax.

Step 1: Firstly, a large strip of cheesecloth is spread on a plane area. Next, pieces of honeycomb are placed right in the middle of the cheesecloth. You don't need to worry if the honeycomb contains impurities like larva or dead bees embedded within it. It will get segregated eventually as the process continues. Finally, the cheesecloth is tied up into a bundle, such that all of the honeycomb pieces are close together inside the cheesecloth. In case the bundle is too large and likely to come open, it can only be fastened by means of cloth clips. It is time to move on to the next step once a snug bundle is prepared.

Step 2: A large container which can hold the cheesecloth bundle well inside is filled with water and kept on the stove. After this, the cheesecloth bundle is placed inside the container with the water. The burner is ignited, while the flame intensity is kept at a medium. Eventually, when the water boils, the beeswax from the honeycomb will melt down and permeate out of the cheesecloth. The impurities that were in the honeycomb will continue to remain inside the cheesecloth. You can observe the melted beeswax floating as a yellow liquid in the water. For best results, it is recommended that the cheesecloth (which is used to hold the honeycomb) will have multiple layers. The beeswax then melts out and will be even more pure. Better filtration will be achieved with the additional number of layers.

Step 3: After almost all the wax seems to have melted out of the bundle, it is time to force the trace amount of beeswax still left in the bundle out into the water. This step will ensure that the maximum possible amount of beeswax has been extracted from the honeycomb. It is recommended the squeezing process to be done with a pair of tongs, since the cheesecloth bundle is likely to be hot in this stage. The cheesecloth bundle may be twisted or pressed or wrung in as many ways possible, so that the maximum amount of beeswax is extracted.

Step 4: The cheesecloth bundle can be taken out of the container after the previous step. The container with the melted wax and water mixture is then allowed to cool. The cooling process may take hours. The beeswax will gradually condense into a thick layer on the top of the water. Once the cooling is complete, the layer of beeswax will solidify as it floats on the water. It will take on a darker shade of yellow color once it solidifies. You need not worry, for if there are some bubbles in the beeswax, they will disappear once it completely solidifies.

Step 5: Once the beeswax has completely solidified, it can be easily taken out of the container by pressing on the edges of the lump of beeswax. It should easily come out of the container without any issues. After the beeswax is taken out of the container, it should be laid on a clean cloth to remove the water still remaining on the surface. After it is completely dried out, you have a pure lump of cleaned beeswax extracted from the honeycomb.

Purification of the beeswax

Even though beeswax candles can be easily purchased in the market, there is some satisfaction in making them on your own at home. Most people are not aware that beeswax candles are excellent air purifiers. The purification process works by the release of negatively charged ions into the surroundings which bind themselves to the positively charged radicals in the air. These positively charged radicals are in the form of dust particles or pollen that are common in the air. Burning beeswax candles supposedly clears all the viruses and bacteria that are floating around in the air. The mechanism by which beeswax candles purify the air around is known as negative ionization. Beeswax candles are a lot healthier than the normal paraffin candles that are cheaply available in the market. Beeswax candles do not release harmful fumes into the surroundings like the other paraffin candles. Making candles at home is a lot easier than most people think, but the beeswax needs to be purified before the candles are made.

Obtaining good quality raw beeswax for candles is not exactly an easy process. That is why it is essential to purify the beeswax before it is made out into candles. No matter what kind of candles are going to be made out of the beeswax, be it scented candles or colored beeswax candles, the process of purifying it is absolutely essential. Most people do not realize that unprocessed beeswax consists of fragments of propolis and other wastes which are not suitable for candle making. This section hopes to shed some light on this aspect, since a lot of people are unaware on how to do it efficiently.

Firstly, the supplies needed for this process need to be kept handy. It requires a double boiler, a finely knit item of clothing - such as a pillow cover, some parchment paper, and a large, heat-resistant container.

Step 1: The beeswax needs to be emptied onto the double boiler. You can utilize a steel bowl in the absence of a double boiler, placing it inside a container containing boiling water. The beeswax is made to melt thoroughly in the container, such that it turns into a total liquid. The process of melting can take some time; however, acceleration may cause sudden overflow. The melting process should be done on a medium heat and must be supervised for safety reasons.

Step 2: Next, the bowl is lined with parchment paper in order to serve as mold for the hot wax when it is poured into the bowl. The fine knit cloth is lined over this parchment paper. The piping hot wax is poured into the bowl once the lining part is complete. The cloth is then lifted off the bowl so that all the waste, including propolis, is segregated from the wax. The cloth should be held over the bowl until the hot wax stops dripping. The hot beeswax should be allowed to cool slowly. The cooling process should happen naturally without any external aid so that it settles well. After it has solidified, the wax hunk can be easily removed by yanking on the parchment paper. The melted beeswax may also be poured into silicon molds after it is purified. This just makes the process of cleaning up after easier. This process can be repeated to further purify the beeswax as needed. The number of times the purification needs to be repeated depends on the source of the beeswax. Cleaner beeswax is usually more expensive. Once the beeswax is thoroughly purified, then it can be used to make immaculate candles.

Although the purification process is not exactly that difficult, cleaning up the bowl after the whole process can be messy. However, there is a trick in order to simplify the cleanup post the filtering. For this, the wax stained bowl is heated to about two hundred degrees Fahrenheit in the oven. After the heating is over, the traces of wax should melt down into liquid which can be easily cleaned with the help of tissue papers. Once the traces of wax are removed, do not forget to wash it neatly with plenty of soap and water.

Melting the beeswax cappings

Most people do not realize that the beeswax is a lot more expensive than honey when taken in equal weights. There are myriad uses for beeswax like in making cosmetics, soap manufacture, waterproofing, candle making and many others. Beeswax has a lot of impurities in it once it is removed from a honeycomb, such as: mud, wooden splinters, cocoons of bees, propolis and many others.

A lot of apiculturists (beekeepers) do not make the effort to salvage and extract the wax from their hives. Only a few backyard apiculturists actually go through the process of rendering the beeswax by melting and refining it.

This is the reason large apiculture enterprises just sell off their cappings and hive wastes to professional wax renderers. Professional wax renderers are able to profitably extract beeswax from these hive wastes. They have invested a lot of money in the equipment, which is specifically made for this purpose. Leveraging this equipment, they easily extract beeswax without creating a mess while doing it. The beeswax melting industry is not as large as the honey making industry. Hence, it is not so well-known among the general public. A lot of beeswax rendering enterprises do not advertise their services. Rather, they are known to apiculturists through grapevine. Some of the larger rendering companies do advertise on various apiculture sites and blogs on the internet. One can find a number of beeswax renderers near them, should they search for them using this method.

The process of melting beeswax cappings begins by removing them from the comb. Thanks to the progress of technology, most apiculturists utilize an electrical heated knife to cut the cappings off from the substrate. This can be done through a normal knife heated by hot water as well. Once the cappings are separated, they are cracked open by means of a roller. The honey obtained by crushing the cappings has tiny bits of wax in it. You need to be wary of this since it is likely to clog the strainer. The honey can still be salvaged by letting the crushed cappings settle in a bucket; then, it perforates to the bottom. A small bucket containing crushed cappings, with a perforated bottom, is hung directly above a larger bucket or pan and left overnight. The next day, all the honey is drained and collected on the larger bucket or pan.

The next step is cleaning the honey-free crushed cappings. Cappings are usually sticky, so they are cleaned using potable water. The cleaning process should be thorough enough to remove all the remaining stickiness and honey. Some apiculturists do this by spreading cappings on a plane surface and letting the bees get rid of the honey in open air. While it has its risks, this is an effective way to clean the cappings.

Finally, the cappings are ready to be melted. The beeswax cappings are delicate and need to be melted slowly. Cappings which are excessively heated lose their natural honey color, as well as their distinguishing aroma. The melting process can be done in a single stage or multiple stages; both are viable. However, the slow melting of cappings is of utmost importance. The process of melting can get messy and should not be done unsupervised.

The process of melting beeswax cappings is best done in ovens. The non-sticky crushed cappings are kept in a container and slowly melted in the oven at the bare minimum setting. Melting will need to go on for hours altogether since it has been placed onto low heat. All the time that goes into slow melting of beeswax will totally be worth it. It results in beeswax which is not only darkish yellow in color, but also gives out a pleasant, sweet honey fragrance. In case you do not have access to an oven, it can also be done using a double boiler. No matter how the beeswax cappings are melted, the key point to be remembered is this: the melting process needs to be done at low heat for several hours.

High quality beeswax feels premium to the touch. It is darkish yellow or orangish in color. Surprisingly, a lot of people have attributed that natural beeswax comes only in a vivid, yellow color. So, quite a lot of them think that the dark yellow or orangish beeswax is adulterated or not pure. It is time that apiculturists educated people regarding this misnomer. Customers might miss out on high quality beeswax just because of the misunderstanding over its color.

Quite a number of beeswax renderers make use of solar melters in order to economically melt the beeswax cappings. Solar melters are usually made out of steel and have a transparent top. This top is covered by a thick glass pane, in order to allow the sun rays to penetrate into the solar melter. The beeswax cappings are kept inside the solar melters and are exposed to the sun for a few days. The heat from the sun will melt them slowly over time. A few of amateur apiculturists make use of Styrofoam containers with glass tops to melt the cappings while using the same principle. The cappings are bundled up in cheesecloth within these Styrofoam melters, so that the pure liquid beeswax that accumulates within the container is kept below the bundle post melting.

One of the ways to pick out high-quality beeswax is by smelling it out. Wax products of other shades of yellow do have the honey fragrance, but they are not as rich or strong as the high-quality wax ones. Melting the beeswax into the liquid form enables it to be used for making candles or molded into any desired shape, simply by pouring it into molds.

Storing your beeswax cappings

Once the process of honey extraction is complete, there arises the problem of storing beeswax cappings until they can be properly processed. All the bits of the honeycomb, along with the cappings, need to be collected. They are precious beeswax. Debris like propolis and others can be easily filtered from beeswax by submerging them in cool water. Lighter constituents like the wax and wood will rise to the top of the surface. Heavier constituents like propolis will sink down to the bottom. After this happens, propolis can be dried up and kept in any normal containers, such as jars.

Beeswax cappings, on the other hand, need to be stored in airtight containers. It is crucial to ensure that there are no wax moth eggs with the cappings. They will consume it upon hatching. If you suspect the presence of such eggs in your wax, then it is advisable to melt it prior to storage. This prevents the wax moths from consuming up the precious beeswax.

Solar wax melters are usually preferred for this, as they are efficient and economical at the same time. The sun will melt the wax and make the process of filtering the beeswax from debris a lot easier. Once the beeswax is melted completely, it can be poured into molds. This gives it a desired shape. Most people prefer Styrofoam containers to hold the beeswax while cooling, as it is easy to remove once it cools down. The melted beeswax is extremely easy to preserve. It can be stored anywhere or even left out. The only pests one may need to worry about are the rats. There is nothing else to worry about if the beeswax is safe from them.

Chapter III: Making Candles Out of Beeswax at Home

Why Should You Use Beeswax?

Nature has bestowed innumerable gifts to mankind; beeswax is a prominent one among them. It is a natural secretion that originates from the wax glands of a honey bees body. The honeybees feed themselves honey in order to stimulate and enhance beeswax production. They huddle together so that the cluster's temperature can go up. The bees need to consume around 10 pounds of honey, however, just to produce a single pound of wax.

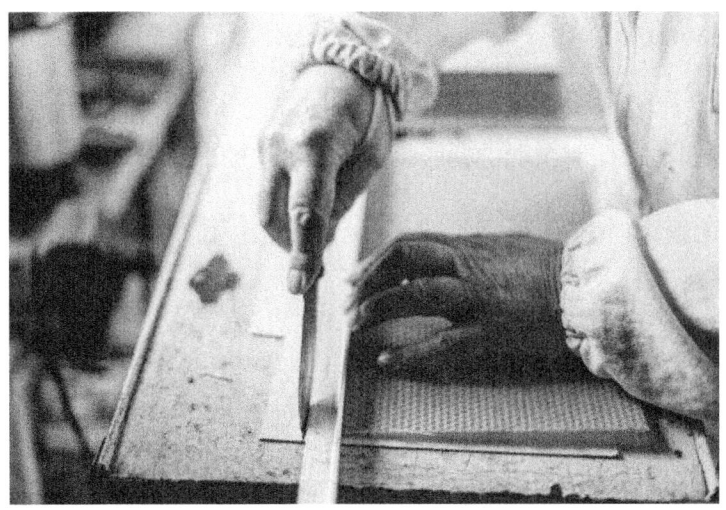

Beeswax is the most natural and purest of all waxes. This conjointly includes the vegetable waxes. Moreover, they do not require any kind of additives and very little processing. You will be surprised to know that this is the only form of wax which can be used in a native state. Only filtering is required for processing. Beeswax candles offer a great ingredient for a healthy house.

Beeswax is also known as bee-wax. Candles made from it burn cleaner, as well as longer, in comparison to ordinary wax candles. They are candles with a natural scent that are made by the honeybees. Although these candles appear to be more expensive when compared to the paraffin candles, they burn so slowly that any kind of price difference can be easily nullified. Beeswax candles are not accompanied by excessive dripping. They emit negative ions when they burn. The end result is the protection of your bodies. It ensures that the air around you is cleaned from particles such as: viruses, mold, toxins, odors, and dust. These are particularly harmful or hazardous for all those people who suffer from conditions such as environmental allergies.

A premium quay beeswax candle will definitely exhibit the following features:

- Its wax is rich and smooth; it is pleasant to touch.

- There is a depth in its finish. There are no cracks, white spots, dark wax or flakes.
- Such candles do not have any visible signs of impurities or dirt.
- Superior quality wicks are used with cotton that has a twist of paper or 100 percent cotton.
- They do not have any kind of cavities or holes to have a negative influence on the burn quality.
- Natural beeswax features a natural honey aroma.

There are so many people who prefer purchasing beeswax candles as compared to paraffin candles. The former is made from a natural product. In fact, these candles are also more appealing to people who religiously practice a vegetarian or vegan lifestyle. You will be happy to know that the honeybees are not at all harmed when beeswax candles are made. It takes about thirty-three million visits for the bees to pollinate flowers which makes only one pound of beeswax; therefore, several people feel that there is a methodology to nature's productivity and a more powerful spiritual connection established by the beeswax candles - as opposed to other kinds of candles. Many of you must be already aware of the immense health benefits facilitated by beeswax candles. This makes them even more alluring to most users.

There are several reasons why beeswax candles are of superior quality. You should definitely switch to them if you're uncertain about them. When you are making up your mind about different candle types, it makes sense to be fully aware of the various health benefits of a beeswax candle. Only then you can easily select candles which are the most appropriate for your health requirements and lifestyle.

Following are some of the top reasons why you should start using beeswax candles:

Beeswax is created by the honey bees
The beeswax candles are created from the wax of bees. It is completely free of chemicals and is 100 percent natural. They are regarded as the oldest candles known to humans. These candles have been prized dearly since the ancient era.
On the contrary, paraffin candles are a bi-product of highly refined petroleum and are oil-based. They may constitute of up to eleven toxic chemicals like toluene and benzene. They also emit exhaust diesel fumes which are highly toxic in nature.

Non-toxic, safe and environmentally fern duly products
Beeswax candles burn clean and emit very little smoke; that is, if they are not based on oil products and are trimmed well. Beeswax candles are 100 percent pure and are completely natural. They are

biodegradable and do not undergo any kind of chemical processing.

In opposition, candles made of paraffin are treated with 100 percent industrial bleach for changing its shade to white while forming toxic dioxins. Acrolyn, a carcinogenic chemical, is added thereafter so the white sludge can be solidified. Eventually, what you get is a highly toxic product. When you burn these candles, you are actually producing the same kind of toxins. In case you are familiar with how poisonous the candles made from paraffin are, it will be natural for you to dump them immediately. The air pollution in your house can be stopped instantly.

Beeswax candles have a great aroma since their natural scent is derived from the floral nectar and honey in the honeycomb. They are also carbon-neutral in nature.

Paraffin candles, on the other hand, constitute of synthetic fragrances and artificial scents. These create stains and toxins when they burn, further causing harm to the environment.

Beeswax candles are known to have a very high melting point
Many experts claim that these candles have the highest melting point among all the known waxes available. It leads to a much longer burn time, which is two to five times higher. They also drip very little or not at all. It is an important feature of beeswax candles, as this fixes the higher expenses associated with them.

However, paraffin candles are not that efficient. Their burning time is lower in comparison and can even drip excessively. It also signifies that these candles will not be economical in the long run. Nonetheless, extra chemicals can be included for lowering their dripping.

Beeswax candles burn brighter and stronger

These candles emit light that is naturally bright and of a light spectrum; which reflects the light of the sun.

Paraffin candles produce flames, which are not as brilliant and strong. However, they are able to evoke a similar natural style of ambiance and warmth as beeswax.

Health benefits of beeswax candles

These candles are beneficial for people suffering from conditions such as: asthma, sensitivities and environmental allergies. It is possible, as they are made from 100 percent natural products and do not emit heavy soot or toxic byproducts when burned.

Things to remember while making beeswax candles

Beeswax candles emit negative ions contrary to artificial waxes. These are helpful in collecting positively charged particles such as chemicals, dust, and dirt in the air. Thus, it is possible to significantly improve your home's air quality just by lighting a beeswax candle. Be that as it may, you need to remember certain important points while making beeswax candles. Check out some of them below:

Keep an eye on a beeswax while it melts

It is important to keep an eye on the wax while it melts due to its inflammable nature. The candle's wax is overheated when it starts smoking. Therefore, you need to keep a tab on that. In fact, it is best to use a double boiler for this purpose.
Likewise, ensure that the wax pellets are not scattered onto a hot stovetop.

Reduce melting point by mixing palm or coconut oil

Although it is possible for you to use only beeswax for the candles, you should remember that its melting point is high. Beeswax has a tendency of tunneling while it burns due to this. While it is not something to be highly concerned about, there could be the formation of a ring from the wax in the jar; this would not burn. The melting point of beeswax comes down when you mix your beeswax with palm or coconut oil; these have a soft texture; thus, beeswax gets hot the entire way.

There is another big merit of adding soft coconut oil to beeswax while making your candles. Beeswax is slightly on the costlier side. In order to reduce its cost without compromising quality of a beeswax candle, the addition of softer oil can stretch your beeswax candle even more. Many experts will suggest you go for coconut oil since it is easily available and inexpensive. The oil also gives your beeswax candles a nutty and fresh scent. This can work quite well with all types of fragrances - anything from rosemary to lavender.

As previously mentioned, you can go for palm oil if it is available to you. Just ensure that you need to double the proportion of this oil from the quantity mentioned in the recipe for coconut oil. Then, mix the oil as usual. Including oil in a beeswax candle will help your candle to burn in a more consistent manner. At the same time, it is imperative for you to note that it is also possible to make 100 percent beeswax candles too as mentioned before.

Choose beeswax granules instead of blocks

There is a word of caution while you purchase your beeswax for making candles. Experts recommend that one should opt for beeswax granules instead of going for blocks. Although the blocks are slightly less costly in comparison to the granules, you have to make it softer by putting it in a microwave oven. It can be a messy affair at the end. These blocks require you to have strong wrists; it is almost impossible for you to chop. Some people have even complained that their knives were about to break into two while they tried to cut the blocks into small pieces. Thus, purchase granules from the market. Save your knives, time and energy.

Handling cracking problems

There have been some reports on cracking issues right at the top of a beeswax candle. Reserve some oil or wax to remelt at a later point in time. You can then pour a second thin layer of it to get a smooth top after it has cooled down.

Ingredients required

Who can refute the fact that beeswax candles smell deliciously good? These candles offer a host of benefits apart from just having aesthetic appeal. They also purify the air while burning in a clean way. Have you wondered where to procure beeswax if you are planning to make these candles at home?

You are really fortunate if there are bee hives stored at your house. Filtered and homegrown beeswax is indeed an excellent choice to make your homemade candles. But, there is a high possibility that you do not have these honeybees at your home. In such a scenario, you can contact the beekeepers in your community to find out whether someone is offering beeswax for sale. If that is not possible, then you can always go to Amazon's website and find out.

What should you know prior to getting started?

Even before you start the experiment of making beeswax candles at your home, you should note that beeswax is highly flammable in nature. Hence, you should not melt the wax on direct heat in a pan. Also, remember to keep a close watch while it is being melted using a double-boiler.

Where can you find all the ingredients required for making beeswax candles?

A soft glow emitted by a candle can offer cozy warmth to your house. Can you enjoy the candlelight charm while being confident that there is an improvement in the indoor air quality?

You can achieve such an ambiance, but definitely not with any standard candle available in the market. After all, most paraffin candles purchased from a store are created using petroleum-based wax. Many studies point out that these candles actually end up releasing toxins into the environment in which humans breathe.

It is a great idea to make your own beeswax candles in the comfort of your home. You can easily make the candles yourself, then gift them to others. It is a simple process of melt and pour.

Basic ingredients to make beeswax candles at home

- Beeswax
- Container for homemade candle
- Double boiler
- Measuring cups, water, and kitchen stove
- Disposable aluminum tin
- Cotton - beaded wick square in shape
- Pencil, pen or scissors

Beeswax

It is a truly exquisite substance that is produced by the honeybees. It is the most important ingredient to make beeswax candles on your own. There is a high likelihood that you cannot make this wax at home by yourself. In such a scenario, you can get in touch with the local beekeepers in your neighborhood to get beeswax for your candles. However, if you do not find one in your locality, you can always go online and buy from sites like Amazon.

Sustainable brand of palm oil

As mentioned earlier, you need to mix either coconut oil or palm oil with beeswax. This helps to make sustainable beeswax candles. The basic aim of mixing palm or coconut oil to it is to drop the melting point of beeswax, as the former has a soft texture. Thus, the candle gets uniformly hot. It also helps in offsetting the cost of beeswax candles. Their quality does not get compromised since the oil stretches the life of these candles. These oils, too, give a nice scent to your beeswax candles. If you are not sure where to look for good quality or sustainable brand of palm oil, then you can go to a good supermarket where authentic products are available. Alternatively, look for it on a renowned website such as Amazon to make an online purchase quite easily.

Wicks

There is a chain of events that take place when you light a beeswax candle. You light the wick with your matchstick and the wick begins to burn. The wax then starts melting due to the wax. The function of a wick is to function as a pipeline since it is a carrier of the melted wax by forming a vapor. This phenomenon is known as capillary action.

Wicks are an essential and key ingredient for making your own beeswax candles.

You need to be careful while procuring wicks for your candle. There are some wicks that allow the quick flow of plenty of fuel through a large pipe. There are others that are slow in pumping fuel through smaller pipes. The flames get either too little or excessive fuel; it will either sputter out or burn poorly. So, you need to select the wick in a manner to ensure that there is a proper balance of flow and fuel.

Essential oils

You need to include essential oils in your beeswax candles for that extra special fragrance to soothe the ambiance. However, you should procure high-quality ones in order to make great candles. There are good wholesale suppliers who have their presence on the internet. You can choose a reputed supplier to get your supply of exquisite essential oils. They offer these at competitive and wholesale prices. For instance, you can try out newdirectionsaromatics.com for procuring high-quality essential oils to make your homemade beeswax candles. New Directions Aromatics is a key supplier that sells products from several leading manufacturers online. It is known to offer fine, pure and natural products.

Weighing scale

Weighing scale is a crucial component for measuring your ingredients for beeswax candles. If your measurement is not accurate, then you may not come up with the desired end product. You can get good weighing scales on Amazon.

Make Sure You Have the Right Equipment for Making Beeswax Candles at Home

Just make sure that you have the right set of equipment at your disposal if you are planning to make candles at home. It is easy to find the following basic supplies and equipment at any craft store or online.

Create a distinct workspace

The first thing you need to ensure is safeguarding your work area. In case you plan to use your kitchen to make candles, all your countertops should be covered well to make sure they are not stained by the dyes that get spilled when you pour the prepared beeswax.

For instance, you may use materials such as wax paper, aluminum foil or newspapers to cover the countertops.

A heat source is also needed to be accessed for melting the wax and function as your work counter. Thus, a kitchen appears to be quite an obvious site. On the other hand, if there is an extra space in your house that you may exclusively use for your candle making projects, then there is a need for equipment like a portable burner and a table.

Look out for a pouring pot

The basic equipment required for making your own container candles is quite simple. The best bet would be to get a pot that you may completely dedicate for making candles at home. It is better not to use the same pot for food. Select a pot made of stainless steel with a preference for a utensil that has a pouring spout.

You may also use some other appropriate container to function as your melting pot. After all, it is not mandatory to melt the wax in an expensive container.

Make your own double boiler

It is advisable to have a double boiler; it is not a good idea to melt the beeswax directly on heat for there is a risk of a fire breakout. Hence, to be extra careful, have some baking soda handy when you melt the wax. The substance can function in the same manner as a fire extinguisher does.

In case there is a wax fire in your kitchen, never try to put it out by using water; it may have a reverse impact. If you do not have a double boiler at your home, and you do not want to spend extra bucks for your candle making DIY project, then it is possible to create a facsimile of a double boiler at your home itself. You can use any medium size stainless-steel pot. You then place three canning rings inside to create a makeshift rack or trivet. For that matter, it is also possible to use any other similar utensil that you already have in your kitchen. The key point you need to remember, and follow, is to have your pouring pot ready. First start pouring water into a base pot. Next, place your pouring pot right on top of those canning rings.

Purchasing wax for candle making

Today, you can find different kinds of wax in the market for candle making. For instance, paraffin wax is available in slabs or beads. It is also possible to purchase container wax that has been specially prepared for candlemaking. It is basically a wax blend. The specially prepared wax is typically formulated to yield less shrinkage and hold more scent. There are a few container waxes available which can be poured only once. It also signifies that there is no requirement for any topping off. However, it is a pricier form of wax blend.

You may be curious to know the actual meaning of topping off. It refers to filling a depression or well that forms around a wick while the wax sets. The top off should be done for a few times so that the well can be filled. You should remember to not fill your container too high initially, since you will be including more wax while you top off.

Get a thermometer

It is possible to purchase designated and dedicated thermometers that are used for making candles at home. However, you may already find an alternative for that available in your own kitchen. For instance, you can also get your job done using a candy thermometer in case you already have one in your home. You need to simply wipe it off properly when your beeswax is warm, so that it can be cleaned quite easily. You need to remember that your beeswax should not be overheated at all; this overheating may even lead to a fire as previously mentioned. The packaging usually includes proper guidelines for temperatures to be maintained just in case you have purchased your wax from a craft store. This includes melting the wax in your kitchen or any other designated area you have chosen. You should make it a point to follow the instructions mentioned on the packages. A majority of "household" waxes, for instance, are known to melt at 130 degrees.

Candlewick

It is possible to purchase an assembled and pre-waxed wire wick, which can make your DIY project of making container candles a cakewalk. Make sure to peruse through the packaging. It is crucial to apply wick of the right size in accordance to the width of your jars that have been already procured.

The wick assemblies in the market are available in different heights. You need to apply "Tacky Wax" so that the wick can be affixed to the jar's bottom. The idea is that the wick does not move around while pouring the beeswax. It is also natural for you to look for some form of implement, so that the wick gets the necessary support before your beeswax can set up. Some people even use butter knives from their kitchens to keep these wicks in proper place.

Recycling or repurposing jar

You can get any kind of jars in the market. You can use old or recycled jars from your kitchen that can serve the purpose instead of purchasing new jars. For example, canning jars can be an excellent option since they are designed to withstand heat. Alternatively, use your recycled jars from the older candles. These come absolutely free of cost. The good news is that you can try out different items to create a homemade candle. However, the container you pick up needs to withstand flame and heat. It also has to have stability for the sake of safety.

Scents

Fragrances that are made for the purposes of candle making can hold their scent well over a period of time. However, that does not mean it is all right for you to use all oil-based fragrances like potpourri oils, perfumes, or essential/natural oils. You should make it a point to include any scent only at the last minute prior to pouring. Otherwise, there is a possibility that your scent will be cooked out.

Dyes

It is possible to purchase your dyes in liquid or solid forms from the market. In order to simplify your pouring, you may use a dropper for both scents and for dyes. Alternatively, you may also use measuring spoons. Some people opt for crayons to bring in the effect of the dye. However, dyes that are specially made for making candles are the best to use.

You need to experiment with various scents and dyes. Begin the process with only small packages of cheap scent and dye designed for candle making. Follow the directions mentioned on the label. It states the specific ounces to be used for every pound of beeswax. You may begin playing with them once you get the hang of it. An excellent idea is to carefully record the proportions and combinations of scents and dyes you use while you are experimenting. You can then recreate based on what you loved the most.

Instructions for making your very own beeswax candles

Most people are unaware of the joys of candle making. The candle making instructions discussed in this section are extremely easy to follow apart from being inspiring. Candle making is a great idea for group activities as well. So, the next time you are at a loss for coming up with group activities, why not consider candle making? Candles do come in handy in a lot of situations, even in today's advanced world. Apart from lighting up a room, it can also be used to decorate places or to make them smell good. Most people do not realize that each and every unique candle is specifically handmade by the chandler. It enables them to express their inner creativity. Not surprisingly, candles still are a popular choice for people who want to give practical and thoughtful gifts to others.

Materials needed

- Pure beeswax slabs

- Double boiler or a large container and another smaller container: for melting the beeswax.
- Pouring cup: Used tin containers or Pyrex glass cups, which have a spout, are usually suitable for candle making. This needs to be heat resistant, since the molten wax will be very hot once it is poured into the mold.
- Popsicle sticks or any stick similar in size: These articles are used to keep the wick in the middle of the candle till it completely solidifies.
- Silicon molds: The molds determine the size and the shape of the finished candles. There are varieties of molds available in the market. Any mold which is heat resistant can be used. Molds made out of metals or rubbers are also available. It is imperative that one knows that slimmer candles burn down quickly in comparison to thicker candles.
- Wick Tabs: These articles are used to keep the wick in the middle of the candle from the bottom end of the mold. The wick needs to be at the middle of the candle, right from the bottom up to the top. Some wick tabs may even come with stickers to be used with container candles.
- Wick: The rule of thumb is this: thicker wick needs to be used in accordance to the greater diameter of the candle. There are varieties of wicks available in the market. Do some research and choose a wick that is the most suitable for your beeswax candles. Wicks that are mismatched with candles can lead to problems later on; so, it is important that the research part is not skipped.

Instructions

Step 1: Evenly apply some lubricant on the inside of the mold. This is an important step since the candle may get stuck in the mold if this is not done. The candles made might have rough patches on its surface if the lubricant is not uniformly coated. Any cooking spray available at the nearest grocery store will serve this purpose. There is no need to buy any kind of specialized lubricant.

Step 2: Once the mold is properly lubricated, place the wick into it. Make sure that the wick remains straight; this can be challenging. It is recommended to use the wick tabs and popsicle sticks suitably to achieve this goal.

Step 3: The beeswax is slowly melted in a double boiler. If one does not have access to a double boiler, then they can melt the beeswax in a water bath. The larger container is filled with some water for this purpose. The smaller container, which contains the beeswax, is kept in the larger container with water and heated.

It is important that you know that beeswax is inflammable. It starts to burn if it is heated beyond one hundred and seventy degrees Celsius. So, for this reason beeswax should never be melted without supervision. Beeswax can be melted in a microwave if people have access to it. In the microwave, the heat setting must be set to low while melting beeswax.

Step 4: Using pure beeswax is recommended for candle making. If you suspect that the beeswax may not be pure, then the melted beeswax can be filtered through a metal sieve prior to pouring it into the mold. Pure beeswax slabs are easily available in the market. The filtration process is usually not needed.

The melted wax is taken into the pouring cup, so that it can be slowly poured into the mold without any disturbance. The wax is slowly poured into the mold once it has arrived at the right temperature for pouring. There should be no air bubbles formed once the wax is in the mold. If any air bubbles form, they can be get rid of by taping the mold at sides. The mold should be allowed to cool down and solidify once it is filled. Note that, the bigger the mold is, the longer the cooling time it needs.

Step 5: The candle can be removed from the mold once it has solidified. Some people suggest keeping the mold in the freezer for a few minutes, as it helps in smooth removal of the candle. But the freezing step is usually not necessary. The wick is trimmed down half an inch once the candle is removed from the mold.

Step 6: The beeswax candle is almost ready for use at this step of the process. Usually, the bottom of the new beeswax candle needs to be smoothed out by rubbing it against a coarse surface.

Some people add a tougher wax coat to the candle surface in order to give it a smooth glossy surface. It makes it last longer when burning. The glazing agents for candles are available in both sprays and liquids. These glazing agents need to be carefully used after reading the instructions with which they came. The usage instructions for the glazing agents may vary with various brands. This process is optional and is usually used by commercial candle makers as a finishing touch.

Chapter IV: The Different Methods of Making Candles

Things to keep in mind while pouring out the wax

Pouring the wax is an important step in candle making. This has to be done with an extremely steady hand. Certain precautions need to be taken before pouring the molten wax into the molds. This section will shed some light on this aspect of candle making.

Heat proof pour cup

It is important to use a heatproof pouring cup to pour the wax into the mold; the wax will be piping hot during the process of pouring. Usually the pour cups are made out of tin or glass and have a spout to facilitate smooth pouring.

Lubricating the mold

It is important that you do not forget to lubricate the mold unless it is a container candle. If you are forgetful, write it up and put it in a place where you can easily keep glancing over. Spray lubricants are usually preferred in beeswax candle making. In case that is not available, cooking sprays will also work for this purpose. Some candle makers are known to use soap; however, this might not work based on the wax being used. So, it is better to rely on regular lubricants. The lubricant needs to be evenly applied throughout the mold, or else it will not be effective. If the mold is not lubricated, then it might be difficult to remove the candle without deforming its shape.

Straight wicks

Wicks remaining straight is an issue even for experienced candle makers. Although any kind of articles can be used for keeping the wick straight (such as popsicle sticks or elastics), it is recommended to use metal stitch holders. They are sturdy and are immune to the hot wax.

The process of pouring the wax into the molds can be started after all the previously discussed safeguards are implemented. The molten wax should be free of any impurities before pouring; metal sieves can be used to ensure this.

It is important to check the temperature with a proper thermometer before pouring the wax. The pouring temperature of the wax differs with different kinds of waxes; and, it needs to be double checked. It is crucial that the molten wax is at the right temperature when it is poured. If the molten wax is slightly too cool, then it can result in jump lines on the candle. This can affect its aesthetic quotient. On the contrary, if the molten wax is slightly too hot, then wax can tunnel through the surrounding wax resulting in sinkholes.

The molten wax needs to be poured into the mold slowly. Utmost care must be taken to prevent splashes or any shakes, in order to ensure an even and blemish free candle. It is imperative to ensure that there are no air bubbles formed during the process of pouring. In case any air bubbles do form for some reason, they need to be immediately dealt with by tapping on the mold externally. The bigger the mold is, then the more time it needs for cooling.

The different types of wicks

Wicks play an important role in ensuring that the candles burn smoothly without any flickering. The characteristics of the wick chosen to be used in a candle have influence on the rate at which the candle burns. We shall discuss the different types of wicks in this section:

Cored wick

Cored wicks are mostly used in candles such as prayer candles, container candles and novelties. They usually need wicks which can support themselves. These wicks are waxed before being used in candle making to boost their durability. These wicks come in three different varieties: cotton, zinc and paper. Out of these three, zinc cored wicks are the most durable.

Flat plaid wick
Flat plaid wicks are used in candles which do not come with containers. These wicks curl up upon being burnt, in order to ensure that the burning happens uniformly along with minimal mushrooming at the end.

Square plaid wick
Square plaid wicks are the wicks of choice when it comes to beeswax candle making. These are also used in pillar candles and taper candles. These wicks bend slightly at the tip when ignited.

HTP wick
This abbreviation stands for high tension paper wicks. These wicks offer higher rigidity, thanks to the paper centerpiece that is weaved into the wick. These wicks come with the advantages of being self-trimming and rigid at the same time. The higher toughness of these wicks offers symmetrical wax pools and lower carbon mushrooming in comparison to the conventional cored wicks. These wicks can be used in paraffin wax candles, vegetable fat candles and gel candles.

Performa coreless wicks
These wicks are made out of cotton. They are deliberately warped to ensure that they do not curl up upon being ignited. These wicks are dependable; they can burn with a sturdy flame, even in troubling conditions.

LX wicks

These wicks are braided in an exclusive manner. They are flat with no cores. However, these wicks do have steadying threads to make them burn efficiently. The steadying threads keep a miniscule curl when the wick is ignited. The flame will be steady and produce little carbon, thereby effectively decreasing the smoke and glimmer. LX wicks are best suited for use in various container candles and pillar candles, as they are constructed for better burning of different kinds of waxes.

RRD wicks

These wicks were pioneered by the manufacturers of the LX line of wicks. These wicks are round and plaid with a cotton core. The cotton core makes sure that the flame gets an uninterrupted supply of fuel and fragrance. The specialty of these wicks is that they do not get congested with the sticky additives that are present in high concentrations. This is common within heavy fragrance candles and prayer candles. These wicks burn steadily and curl slightly.

This is the most popular wick among most candle makers, for it is good for use with both soy wax and paraffin.

CD wicks

These are similar to the HTP threads; they, too, have a paper centerpiece weaved into the wick. These wicks do not have any cores. They are flat plaid with paper strands twined around it. These wicks are constructed for steady and large flames. These wicks are extremely adaptable. They are best-suited for difficult-to-melt wax candles, such as vegetable fat candles and paraffin candles.

Zinc

These wicks are basically cotton plaid with zinc core concealed in the middle. What's unique about these wicks is that they offer excellent stiffness whenever used in the hot pour procedure. The drawbacks are that these wicks are highly susceptible to mushrooming and carbon amassment. These are usually used in container candles made out of paraffin wax.

How to choose the right wick for your candle?

Choosing the right candle wick is not unimportant just because it is done last. No matter how premium the fragrance of the candle, or from what quality wax the candles are made, the candle will not burn properly if it lacks the right wick. Consequently, candles which do not burn well are less likely to be bought again. It is imperative that you realize the characteristics of the perfect candle wick. Ideally, the wick should be able to burn with a constant flame size. The wick should not burn either too quickly or with high heat, since the container can get charred. This can be a fire hazard. The lesser the carbon deposits it makes, the more suitable the wick is for candle making. Lastly, the wick should glow slightly and not exaggeratedly once the candle is extinguished.

There is no dearth of choices in the market for candle wicks. This is good news for the people making candles, as they can easily choose the best wick without much deliberation. You should know that one particular wick will not serve all the needs. It needs to be carefully thought over before selection. In fact, there are about three hundred different kinds of wicks available out in the market. The perfect wick for a particular case depends on the quantity of the fragrance being used, the thickness of the candles, the pigments which give the candles color and finally, the wax being used to make the candles.

As stated before, wick selection for candles is an important aspect of candle making. The perfect wick makes the candle burn calmly and uniformly without producing any smoke. Most people are unaware that the premium wicks are usually plaited while the more economical ones are typically twined. The rate at which the candle burns depends on the size of the wick. Smaller wicks will burn with smaller flames; therefore, they melt the wax gently. However, this increases the probability of the candle extinguishing it out by itself. On the contrary, a larger wick will burn with a larger flame and melt the wax way too quickly which will most likely subdue the flame.

Factors include the thickness of the candle, the variety of wax used, adulterants like fragrance and pigment, as well as the presence or absence of containers. All play an important role in determining the kind of wick to be used. It is imperative that you know that candles of the same diameter but made out of different waxes need different wicks. Say, for example, it is a fact that beeswax candles need bulky and stiff wicks in contrast to the paraffin candles of the same thickness. All the different varieties of wicks can be categorized into three different kinds based on its shape. They are flat shaped, square shaped and cored.

Flat wicks are utilized in cone-shaped candles, thin pillar candles and prayer candles. The specialty of flat wicks is that they are self-trimming. They burn steadily without any popping. Flat wicks do not need manual trimming by hand and extinguish themselves out.

Squared wicks are plaited to take the shape of square. Usually these are the stiffest kind of wicks. These types of wicks are used in cone-shaped candles, novelty candles and other extra thick candles. All thick candles use square-shaped wicks because they burn with large flames. This lowers the likelihood of uneven melting of candles.

Cored wicks are comprised of a centerpiece made out of lead. Although these kinds of wicks are banned in the US, they are still used in certain parts of the world. Alternatively, cored wicks are now made out of zinc cores. They are covered with paper or cotton threads, which are plaid to give it the characteristic round shape. Among all the other shapes, cored wicks are the sturdiest. It is imperative that you know cored wicks need to be trimmed manually; do not curl these wicks once the wick is burnt. Cored wicks are used in small to medium sized candles such as prayer candles, pillars, floaters, tea candles and other container candles. Wicks with metal cores burn at higher temperatures; consequently, it makes these wicks ideal to be used in gel candles. They need a lot more heat to melt than regular paraffin candles.

Add a little fragrance by making your beeswax candles with essential oils

The benefits that beeswax candles offer do not stop just with brilliant glow and extended burn life. It exudes a mild sweet honey fragrance, instead of the various carcinogenic fumes that other paraffin candles give out while burning. Making beeswax candles at home is a satisfying experience, whether these candles are to be gifted or intended for personal use.

Beeswax candles can be made even better by adding essential oils to it. Beeswax is not good at retaining scent like the other waxes; thus, it is recommended to add coconut oil in order to make the fragrance long lasting.

Even though coconut oil does extend the life of the fragrance in beeswax candles, it does not prolong it satisfactorily for milder fragrances. So, most professional beeswax candle makers stick to using strong fragrances.

It is difficult to pinpoint why the fragrances emanating from the beeswax candles may not be strong enough. It may have to do with the choice of oil and beeswax. Not all essential oils blend with beeswax well. Also, in order to ensure best results, the essential oils need to be added at specific temperatures for them to be effective. Some oils cannot withstand high heat, so the temperature of the melted wax at which they are added becomes important.

Making colored beeswax candles

Beeswax candles are worth every extra penny. They do not pollute the air around them, but rather purify the air while burning. Beeswax candles give out negatively charged ions when they are burnt, which effectively eliminates dirt, allergens and mold which we unknowingly breathe. The usage of beeswax is not limited to candles alone; there are plenty of other uses for it. The process of adding color to beeswax is the easiest part of beeswax candle making. This is something which does not require special training. It can be done well by any average person.

There are three ways in which color can be added to beeswax. They are:

- Liquid dyes
- Color chips
- Crayons

Various liquid dyes are available in the market; you can easily find any color you choose. The liquid dyes are extremely concentrated and should be used carefully. Ideally, seven drops of liquid dye should be mixed with a pound of beeswax in order to give it a moderate shade. The number of drops per pound of beeswax can be increased if desired, but you should ensure that the total number of drops does not exceed fourteen per pound of beeswax. Anything higher than this will get in the way of candle burning.

Color chips are also easily available in the market. More often than not, a single unit of color chip should be sufficient to color one pound of beeswax. However, this fact should to be verified with the individual brand of color chip makers that you choose.

Crayons are the most popular choice for coloring beeswax. Regular crayons are available in most shops and they are ideal for this purpose. Naturally, the beeswax will take up the color of the crayon, so if different shades are needed, then two or more crayons need to be blended together. The ratio of crayons to beeswax blended should be fifty-fifty in terms of weight. Each ounce of colored beeswax comprises of half an ounce of beeswax and half an ounce of crayon.

The mixture of beeswax and any of the dying agents formerly mentioned need to be taken in a glass jar in the appropriate ratio. The glass jar is then heated by means of a water bath to heat it uniformly. Once the beeswax melts, the mixture should be stirred appropriately to blend the color uniformly. Next, the blended beeswax can be used to make molded candles or dipped candles. If the candles need to be thick, then molded candles are the way to go. If the candles need to be slim and lengthy, then dipped candles are a better choice. It is imperative that you remember that molded candles take longer to complete.

In order to make molded candles, the mold should be properly lubricated. This ensures that the candle does not stick to it after it cools. The blended wax is then poured into the lubricated mold slowly with a steady hand. Finally, the wick is added at the end when the mold is filled with molten wax. The molds are set aside for some time to allow it to cool.

A small weight needs to be appended to one end of the wick in order to make dipped candles. The weight is then carefully lowered into the blended liquid beeswax. The wick is held in this position for a few minutes. Then, it is lifted out of the melted beeswax and dipped into it again. This process of dipping the weighted wick is repeated until the candles reach the desired thickness.

Painting your homemade candles: Materials and techniques

People complain that these ready-made candles lack that personal touch in them, even though there are ample varieties of candles available in the market. This section hopes to aid people in imparting that personal touch to their candles. The challenge in painting on candles is making the paint stick to the candle's glossy exterior.

Regular art paints do not adhere well to the wax. Gluing paper with designs painted on them is not viable, as the paper itself is combustible. But you need not lose hope, because painting on candles is not an extremely complicated exercise. It's possible thanks to the availability of candle medium. Blending the candle medium with art paints enables people to paint their own art onto the candles and utilize them for decorative purposes. In this section, we shall discuss three different candle painting techniques, so that you can choose the one most suitable method to imprint your art on your candles. It might take a few trials to get the hang of these techniques.

Conventional painting

At times, it can be extremely difficult to find candles that will go well with the project. People want to use them for a variety of purposes. Even though varieties of candles are available in the market, they might not always be available in the color people want. However, it is not so difficult to find acrylic paints of various colors and shades. Utilizing acrylic paints, people can paint their candles with a color scheme and design pattern of their own choosing.

Materials needed

- Acrylic paints
- Paint brushes
- Palette candle medium
- Cotton pads
- Rubbing alcohol

Step 1: The cotton pads are dabbed with rubbing alcohol and are used to wipe the candles clean. It is imperative to ensure that candle surface has no dust or fingerprints prior to painting. The wiping will get rid of the sheen. This enables the paint to stick to the wax better.

Step 2: The candle medium and acrylic paint are taken in the palette and mixed well. Both the ingredients need to be blended in equal proportions. The blending can be done with paint brushes and must be thorough.

Step 3: Using the mixture prepared and the paint brushes, the candles can be painted as desired. The paint should be completely dry before the candle can be touched, or another color is painted over the first coat. Multiple coats may be necessary to get the desired shade of color.

Using paper transfer technique

To those who are uninitiated, transfer paper is a fine paper which is painted with pigments via a hand or printers. It is used to imprint the design on substrates. At times, heat presses may be leveraged to make the transfer well. Transfer paper has long been used in printing art on clothing and other art projects. This method can be used to paint on any candles as long they are not container candles.

Materials needed

- Tissue paper
- Conventional printer paper
- Printer
- Wax paper
- Blow dryer
- Adhesive
- Adhesive tape

Step 1: The tissue paper is taped to the conventional printer paper. Then, it is fed into a printer so that the desired design pattern is printed onto the tissue paper.

Step 2: The printed tissue paper is gently wrapped around the candle. Only the image part is cut out of the whole tissue paper if just an image is to be transferred.

Step 3: The tissue paper is then stuck onto the candle. This eliminates any wrinkles or gaps between the candle surface and the printed tissue paper. Adhesive may be used for this purpose.

Step 4: The candle is wrapped with wax paper once the printed tissue paper is stuck on the candle surface. Next, the blow dryer is used to impart heat to the wax paper. The wax will heat up and absorb the tissue paper once it sufficiently heats up. The wax paper can be removed after the heating process is uniformly completed within a few minutes. It is important that the candle is allowed to dry up after removing the wax paper.

Making streaked candles

Streaked artworks are in vogue nowadays. Decorating with streaked candles will significantly up the aesthetic quotient of even the dullest living spaces. In this part we shall discuss a twirling method to impart a streaked look to your candles.

Materials needed

- Paper towels
- Large serving spoon or stick
- Oil paints (Two or three contrasting colors are recommended)
- Water
- Gloves
- Nail polish remover
- Large bucket.

Step 1: The bucket is filled with clear water so that the candles can be easily immersed in it. The paint vials are shaken well to get rid of any sedimentation. Then, a few drops of the color are added to the water. Few drops of other colors may also be added in the same fashion. The serving spoon is used to spin the paint around the water surface. Note that the streaking effect may not be pleasant if more than three colors are used; be wary of this fact.

Step 2: The candle is nimbly held by its wick and is dipped fully into the water. The immersing of the candle should be done at a slow pace while moving the candle in a circle. The residual paint on the water surface needs to be removed via the paper towels prior to removing the candle from the water. This is done to prevent the candle from taking on a second layer of color. Once the candle is removed, it should be gently swayed to get rid of surplus water.

Step 3: Once the candle stops dripping, it should be dried either by keeping it on a candlestick or by hanging by its wick. The streaked candles are ready to be used after they are finished drying. This process can be repeated for other candles as well. It is important that all of the remaining paint is removed prior to adding fresh paint into the water.

A few ideas on decorating your homemade beeswax candles

People want innovative ideas to spruce up their living spaces and they are constantly in search for them. Decorative candles are all the rage right now; there is no limit to the way they can be used to increase the aesthetic quotient of any kind of living space. Apart from using them for decoration, decorative candles also serve as great gifts for friends and loved ones. There is no dearth of techniques to decorate beeswax candles. The choices are only limited by the effect people want to achieve. It does not matter if candles are homemade or bought from the market; any kind of beeswax candles can be easily decorated. In this section we shall discuss some ideas on how to decorate beeswax candles.

Sticking wax cut-outs: Colorful wax sheets are available in all the craft shops. These wax sheets can be utilized in a variety of ways. They can be impressed upon by using seals or cut into various shapes. These wax cut-outs can then be stuck onto beeswax candles to decorate them. There are wide range of seals and shape cutters available in craft stores for this purpose. If one is skilled enough, they can carve their own cut-outs by using knives.

The wax cut-outs can be stuck onto the surface of beeswax candles once they are ready; this is done by heating them up through a blow dryer and pressing them once they soften up.

Painting on the candles directly: One need not be an artist to paint eye-catching art on the surface of beeswax candles. Anyone can make an ordinary beeswax candle look extraordinary simply by using markers and glitter gels. Painting out different shapes and patterns can also significantly improve the aesthetic quotient of the beeswax candles. The designs and motifs can be derived from the occasion for which candles are going to be used, such as a Christmas tree for Christmas decorations or hearts and teddy bears for Valentine's Day. Using multiple colors which complement each other well will make the candles stand out.

Fire n' ice candles: Beeswax candles can easily be given a frozen effect. In order to achieve this, one needs to proportionally mix Epsom salts with pigments in a cup. The pigment should be based on the shade of the color needed. This mixture is to be put in drops on a plate so that it forms a thin layer. Next, a paint brush is taken and dipped in craft glue. Then, the requisite designs are painted on the candle. Once the designs are complete, the candles are rolled onto the plate containing Epsom salts mixture. The candles need to be rolled onto the mixture, while the glue is still wet or else it will not work. There are no restrictions to the designs that can be made.

Potpourri candles: Potpourris are famous all over the world for their unique mild fragrance. Using dried flowers and fruits to decorate beeswax candles is fairly simple. The dehydrated fruits and flowers need to be cut into thin slices before they can be stuck onto the candles. It is advisable to use non-toxic adhesive for this purpose. The elements of the potpourri can be arranged as one desires. It is important not to forget to dip the candles in clear melted wax while making potpourri candles; after all, the slices are stuck. This allows them to stay intact for long periods of time. Potpourri candles are sure to be the cynosure of all guests who come to your home.

Chapter V: Fun Recipes to Try Out While Making Candles at Home

There are various fun ways to create your own candles at home. However, the finest and most important step for any candle making process is to know and procure the essential ingredients. Read on to know some fun recipes for making your own beeswax candles.

Recipe for lavender candles

Lavender is the favorite scent for many people all around the world. It is, after all, an herbal and floral fragrance having balsamic undertones. If you are one of the innumerable admirers of this fragrance, then using lavender candles at your home is one of the simplest ways to spread its intoxicating scent throughout your house.

Many experienced people will tell you that dried lavender is not as effective as burning lavender candles at your home. The former does not spread as uniformly and quickly as a burning beeswax candle with lavender fragrance. However, good beeswax candles with superior quality fragrance can be pretty costly. Fortunately, you can make your own lavender candles at home.

Yet, here is a note of caution before you learn this fun recipe. Avoid adding lavender buds to your homemade candles since they can easily catch fire when your candle burns down. It is better not to add the buds for avoiding risks like these. So, you need to skip this step while making candles at home.

Supplies or ingredients required

You do not require plenty of supplies to make your own lavender candles. Check out the ingredients you will need below:

- Candle beeswax
- Candle Wicks
- Essential lavender oil
- Glass containers
- Candle Dye

You can find these supplies for your candles at a craft store in your locality or online.

Steps for making these candles

Step 1: Place the parchment under the jars so that they can catch any spilling wax. The candle wicks' bottom should be hot glued to the glass jars' bottoms while ensuring that the wicks are placed in the middle of the jar. You need to ensure that your wick spreads a minimum of half inches above from the top of beeswax.

Step 2: Take a double boiler and melt about two to three pounds of candle beeswax in it. Keep the flame of the burner at a medium-high or medium level. Allow the melted wax to rise to a temperature of about 180 degrees.

Step 3: Now turn off the burner and allow the wax to cool to about 125 degrees. Next, add around five ounces of high-quality lavender oil for each two to three pounds of your candle beeswax. You should add dye now if you want to use it. For instance, you can add an equal but small proportion of red and blue candle dye for achieving a soft, lavender hue. It is recommended to include a small portion of dye at a single point of time till you get the right shade. The reason is this: it is not possible to go back if the color is too dark. There is no need to use lavender buds. The candles will smell great despite not adding them. Be careful while pouring the beeswax into the containers. You can use a funnel to be sure about the wax not spilling at all.

Step 4: Allow your lavender beeswax candles to cool for the entire night. Then, trim the wicks to about one-fourth inches above the candle. You can either reuse your old jelly jars or use brand new glass jars to place your lavender beeswax candles. How about decorating the lids of these jars and giving these candles to your dear ones as gifts? You can also keep them with you to decorate your rooms. Lavender has a soothing smell. Your home will smell heavenly when you burn these candles.

Recipe for homemade crayon candles

It has been observed that candles made at home can cost only a few bucks. Still, they can burn and smell as good as the costly ones available in the markets. In fact, a candle making project is quite an easy project since it only takes more than a few hours to complete. These candles are excellent additions to your den or workspace. They can even act as great DIY and inexpensive gifts for your dear ones.

There are different kinds of beeswax candles that you can make at home. But, this fun recipe is about making crayon candles at home.

Steps for preparing crayon candles at home

Step 1: Collect your materials or ingredients for making a crayon candle. Several crayons of different colors will be required in order to make this candle. You will also need a container to melt those crayons. For example, you can use cup liners made of aluminum in an old cake pan. Just be sure that it does not have any pores through which the wax may leak. You will also require a candle wick, a recycled or a new jar and a few Popsicle sticks for stirring.

Step 2: Begin the candle making process by setting an oven to a temperature range of 220 to 265 degrees. Do not be in a hurry to set its temperature too high since the oven can then become excessively hot. Our recommendation is to begin with a relatively lower temperature and then do adjustments accordingly.

Step 3: Your next step should be peeling off the paper from the purchased lot of crayons. Then, break them into tiny pieces. You can use about seven to ten different crayons of every color for your homemade crayon candle.

Step 4: Let the crayons melt. Add them to the melted beeswax.

Step 5: Place the candle wick in a jar and hold onto it while you keep pouring the mixture into that new or reused jar. You may wrap the wick around one of the Popsicle sticks if it is too long. You can then place that stick across your jar so that it can be kept in place well.

Step 6: The beeswax must be allowed to set for some time prior to adding another color.

Step 7: You need to continue adding different colors while allowing each color getting set.

Step 8: The wick needs to be firm after all the colors have been added and then set.

When you light this beautiful candle, you will find that it burns well for approximately 15 minutes. Thereafter, the flame will become smaller and smaller. You will definitely love the way the crayons smell. It is a beautiful DIY project for making a pretty and decorative candle that is all about melting and mixing different colors. However, you need to note that this crayon candle is not something you should use for emergencies.

Fun recipe for making beeswax candles with forest scents (essential oils)

Many people have a great affinity towards pure beeswax candles when they shop for air purifiers for their homes. These candles have a sweet fragrance and a cozy glow. However, what is even more interesting is that they are known for the ability to emit negative ions in the air where they burn. These ions can lend a sunny and uplifting gleam to a room and improve the quality of air. Pure beeswax candles are also devoid of toxic chemicals that are usually common in many conventional candles. Candles made from pure beeswax, in fact, burn more cleanly as compared to other waxes. Beeswax, as mentioned earlier, features a higher melting point and that helps it burn for a longer time period.

Ingredients or supplies for forest scented beeswax candles

You need to mix these essential oils to four ounces of beeswax in a melted form:

- Cypress - 15 drops
- Juniper Berry - 15 drops
- Douglas Fir - 25 drops
- Atlas Cedar - 25 drops

Ingredients for making woods scented beeswax candle

Include all the below-mentioned essential oils to about four ounces of beeswax in a melted form:

- Sweet Orange - 5 drops
- Lavender - 10 drops
- Black Spruce - 15 drops
- Frankincense - 25 drops
- Norway Pine - 25 drops

Essential oils of superior quality can be purchased quite easily from a number of online reputable suppliers.

Other important points to note before making beeswax candles with forest scents:

Preferably, contact a local beekeeper to procure your supplies of beeswax for making candles at home

Local beekeepers raise honey bees through organic procedures. They are passionate about their beekeeping most of the time. In comparison, commercialized beeswax is usually harvested unsustainably. It is important for you to be conscious while sourcing your beeswax for DIY candle making at homes. Additionally, when you show your support for these small-scale beekeepers by purchasing waxes from them, you are actually helping these people to establish and build healthy beehives. This can produce healthier honeybees. However, if you do not find beekeepers in your locality, you can take the help of a credible online supplier such as Amazon to source your beeswax.

Make use of a good quality crockpot

Beeswax has a high melting point, so it is important to keep a close vigil on it while heating the wax on a stove. It also means that someone has to stay in a kitchen for quite some time. You can use a crockpot, setting it to high for about four to six hours and let it melt. You should not put a lid on this crockpot or else there could be water in your wax while air bubbles will get inside your candles. These candles, as a direct result, will be burning unevenly. After the beeswax gets melted, a potholder can be used in order to take out the jar from the crockpot. Make sure that you dry the bottom properly and then pour the wax carefully into the prepared jars. You can either go for beeswax coated or organic cotton wicks for your candles as they work quite beautifully.

Fun recipe for making DIY coffee candles

Making a coffee candle at home can be both exciting and fun at the same time. Check out the detailed step-wise recipe for making coffee candles at home.

Preparations or ingredients

- Used or old beeswax candles
- Beer/cider can

- A pot with handle
- Empty tin/container
- Ground coffee
- Salvaged candle wicks
- Teaspoon

How to get started?

The first step would be to remove the can's top so that you get your makeshift wax melting pot. Next, collect all your old candles and tea lights in one place. Shove them all into that can. Ensure that the wicks are rescued. You are now all ready to pour water into the actual pot. Make it almost half full and also ensure that it is under a boil temperature. You need to place the melting pot into that water and then observe the beeswax getting melted.

Wax making procedure

The wax will be in a liquid state after about three to four minutes. You need to ensure that you use a teaspoon to stir continuously so that the entire wax gets liquefied properly. You need to make your "melting pot" in the shape of a jug. You can do this by pinching one of its sides.

Time for adding the coffee

You can use a strong ground espresso coffee. The reason for including this is that you would not be able to smell the coffee unless it is that strong. You can add about two teaspoons of the coffee to mix with the melted beeswax. Try to dissolve the mixture by boiling them together. You can leave some coffee granules intact since they will enhance the effect of your coffee candles at the end.

Make your DIY candle now

It is a very simple step to follow. You can use your straining board to bring the beeswax to the surface very quickly. Next, you need to prepare your container to pour the mix. You can use your used cookie tin to create this container very easily. In fact, most kitchens will have a tin like this.

Begin the pouring process

The coffee and beeswax mixture should now be poured very carefully into your tin container. You should pour it with great caution because the beeswax is now very hot. You need to put those salvaged wicks very quickly into your candle prior to it setting down. You can use the wicks from your standard tea lights as mentioned earlier.

Your coffee candle is ready now

You need to allow it to set and marvel at what you finally got after all your efforts. You can get a nice scent of coffee from the candle once you leave the solution to rest for some time. Finally, you can enjoy a nutty warm aroma when you light your coffee flavored beeswax candle.

The entire process of this funky coffee-flavored beeswax candle is actually very simple to follow. The end result will be quite satisfying for you to say the least.

Fun recipe for making DIY Aromatherapy beeswax candles

You may find it pleasantly surprising that aromatherapy beeswax candles are extremely easy and simple to make as a DIY project at your home. You can even use them as an inexpensive but adorable gift to your loved ones. Many people love collecting candles. They believe that, when lit, they have the ability to transform the mood of the people present in that room. The sweet fragrance that wafts through the air and the flicker of the gentle glow can actually bring about quite a soothing effect. Hence, make your own beeswax candles at home since they are easy and cheap. You will feel good when you see the end result of your work. Moreover, these candles do not comprise of any harmful or toxic chemicals. Nor do they compromise any artificial or synthetic scents. The best part is making them and gifting them to your loved ones.

How to select the right quality of essential oils for your homemade aromatherapy candles?

The advocates of aromatherapy will tell you that it is a brilliant way to assist you in enhancing your mental, emotional and physical health. Knowledge of essential oil on your moods will definitely make you even more excited to try your best to make those DIY aromatherapy beeswax candles at your home.

While there are endless ways to make different varieties of beeswax candles at home, this is a very easy recipe. You can source beeswax from local farmers or from a website, as well as a cotton wick and essential oils. Thus, the ingredients needed are minimal and simple.

Ingredients or supplies needed

- A clean can where you will melt the oils
- Cotton Wicks
- Pot
- Wooden stick or spoon to stir
- Essential oils
- Organic or pure form of beeswax

Steps for aromatherapy homemade candles are as follows

Step 1: A double boiler should be created first. You can do so by pouring water into any pot; then, bring it to a boiling stage.

Step 2: Put the beeswax into a can. Position it into the water until the wax melts.

Step 3: As the beeswax is melting, you can use that time to cut the wicks. This will make it possible for the wicks to fit well into a clean mason jar, glass votives and tins. You need to tape them around a pencil.

Step 4: You need to take the beeswax out of the water once it has melted well; mix in the essential oils while stirring it. The stirring should be done continuously, allowing the wax and the essential oils to mix properly and uniformly. How much essential oils you will add to the melted beeswax will depend on the intensity and the strength of the scent which you want in your candles. Some people like to go on mixing essential oils until they can sense a distinct fragrance.

Step 5: Finally, pour the mixture into your prepared containers. Let it cool for some time.

All you need to do now is make beautiful aromatherapy beeswax candles at home. Wasn't the procedure short and simple? There are many people who are a bit hesitant to try this out; they feel that any craft requires lots of creativity and imagination. However, you just saw that is not applicable - at least in the case of aromatherapy beeswax candles.

Scented holiday candles with multiple layers

Ingredients or supplies required

- Beeswax pellets or flakes
- Small pans
- Crayons
- Candle Wick
- Essential oils

Step 1: First, you need to melt the beeswax flakes. Make sure you melt them in small batches since every layer has to cool entirely before you add the next one. When the beeswax has melted fully, pour your essential oils you desire into the pan and keep it stirring with a Popsicle stick or a wooden spoon. You can choose different types of essential oils, such as balsam fir for creating the green layer, clove plus cinnamon for creating the red color, vanilla for creating the white color or sweet orange for producing the pink color. Five to ten drops of each color should be used for every layer.

Step 2: You next step is to place the wick to a jar's bottom by taking a small amount of melted wax. You need to keep the wick at the center by wrapping the top around either a skewer or a chopstick. Now pour your chosen first layer into that jar. Allow it to cool completely. This entire procedure may take about one hour or even more, based on your room temperature. In order to make the process faster, place them either in your refrigerator or outside. That, however, can affect the manner in which the beeswax sets. It is recommended to let them cool down at your room temperature when you want to accomplish an even layer without cracking or bubbling.

Step 3: The process should be repeated with other scents and layers. This gives each leach layer time to fully cool prior to adding the next.

Finally, trim those candle wicks to make sure that there is roughly about half to one-fourth inch left at the top to properly light it. You can top the jar with a lid and store it well until you are prepared to gift it or use it yourself.

Recipe for DIY French Vanilla candle with coffee beans

Every year, it is time to make your home feel warm and cozy with the advent of fall. When the scorching heat of the summer disappears, you feel more than willing to turn on your oven once again to bake that delicious pie. Fall is also the time when the sun sets earlier. People love lighting up their fireplaces in the cold evenings. Even if you do not have a fireplace at your home, lighting up some scented candles is the second-best thing to do. Here you will learn how to add vanilla and coffee beans into these beeswax candles. The fragrance is so sweet that you will feel like eating them up.

You may be surprised, but candle making as a DIY project is a deceptively easy craft. The maximum you need to do is melt and then pour. It is great fun to mix several items up by including texture (such as ice) and using a used can (such as a paint can). Unlike synthetic or artificial flavored candles, candles with natural fragrances are homey, nutty and warm. They do not have an overwhelming scent.

Supplies or ingredients needed

- Chopped vanilla beans
- Coffee beans

- Candle Wick
- Beeswax - You can chop off an old candle at home with no scents, thus recycling the beeswax. Alternatively, you may also purchase wax chips from the craft store.
- Small glasses or bowls - you can easily get pretty cups or bowls in your kitchen.

Steps

Step 1: Start the process by using a microwave-safe bowl or a double boiler to melt the beeswax.

Step 2: Next, glue the candle wick firmly in place of the cup's bottom. You can also hold it with your hand to position it in place at the top.

Step 3: You should then pour beeswax into it to form a small layer. Add another layer of vanilla beans and coffee beans.

Step 4: Fill the remaining portion of the cup with beeswax. Keep stirring the beeswax with a spoon or a chopstick so that the beans can get evenly distributed, if required.

Step 5: Finally, allow the beeswax to harden and then trim the wick.

Step 6: You can fill up many tinted glass cups, which may be easily available. They will look very pretty and do wonders for your table decorations.

These candles look very pretty and adorable. You must try this out as your next DIY candle making project at home.

Now, it is easy to make your house smell like delicious French vanilla. After all, this project is not only delicious but is simple at the same time. All you need to do is grab a bowl, fill it with your favorite coffee beans and melt your beeswax. When you light the candle, the heat emitted from it will make the beans warm. Your entire home will start smelling like a delicious French vanilla cappuccino.

Recipe for homemade Eucalyptus candles with essential oils

Do you love making candles at home like innumerable other people around the world? Candle making does not need a lot of imagination or creativity, as opposed to many other crafts. In reality, making these candles is so simple that you can use used containers and essential oils that you have in your kitchen. When you burn beeswax candles at home, they not only produce a pleasant scent but also burn clean. Plus, they can last for a longer time period.

Eucalyptus candles are ideal for burning in all seasons of the year. These candles offer all the merits that are usually associated with eucalyptus oil. So, are you all set to make these candles on your own? It will come as a pleasant surprise to you that no fancy equipment is required for doing so.

Supplies or ingredients required

- Eucalyptus Essential oil - 10 to 15 drops
- Chopstick or pencil
- Candle Wick measuring minimum six inches or even more than that with weighted base
- One green-colored crayon
- Two and a half cups of beeswax candle flakes
- Canning jars measuring 16 ounces

In order to make any colored candles, you can use crayons for dying your candles. They are cheap and easy to use. Make your candles even more colorful by adding more crayons. In this particular fun recipe, you will be using about half of a crayon since a lighter tint will suffice.

Are you ready to start?

Step 1: Begin the process by first heating the beeswax flakes in a pan made of Teflon on medium heat. You need to ensure that the flakes are moved continuously to prevent clumping or sticking. The heat should be further lowered once the flakes get liquefied. You should then put the crayon's broken pieces into that liquid. Keep stirring to make sure that the color of the crayon gets distributed evenly. You need to now remove the pan from the heat and keep aside. It is precisely the time when you should start adding drops of the eucalyptus oil. You will sense an amazing smell at this moment.

Step 2: Next, wrap both the ends of your candle wick on a chopstick or a pencil. Let this weight drop to the jar's bottom. Use the stick for holding the candle wick in proper place right at the top.

Step 3: Pour the melted beeswax flakes into a jar gradually. You can adjust your wick, if required, since you want it to stay in the center.

Step 4: Keep your jar in a cool site, so that it will have the time and the necessary temperature to solidify. The process of solidification takes about four hours or so on an average. It should not be disturbed before the end of four hours. If you do that, although it may appear hardened from outside, the candle's inside may be still soft. Try not to shake, touch or fuss with it.

Step 5: Take a pair of scissors and cut the candle wick down so that it is approximately half an inch long. Your candle is now all set to be lit and enjoyed by you and your dear ones.

Doesn't the above recipe sound good? So, it is time for you to try out this wonderful candle recipe with eucalyptus essential oil soon. It is easy to make, has a wonderful scent and is amazing to look at.

Fun recipe for making votive candles at home

The section will teach you how to create your own votive beeswax candles. These candles have a classic wedding flavor attached to them. However, they may look boring to some if they are simply bought from stores and are not handmade. A bride who loves making DIY candles will be absolutely thrilled when she learns how to make these candles. After all, these tiny votives are quite simple to make. This candle making project is simply a melt and pour process like many other homemade candle making recipes. Plus, you also get to opt for your own fragrance and color.

Supplies or ingredients required

- Fragrance
- Flutter Dyes
- Wick pins
- Votive Molds
- Wicks
- Old wooden spoon to stir
- Pouring Pot
- Beeswax can be procured from beekeepers or online

These waxes are both unique and beautiful at the same time. They are simple to work with and can melt wonderfully at the same time. Each of these candles has a distinct appearance such as marbled, feathered and crystal. These colors give the votives quite a rustic appearance. They look charming due to their unique lines and imperfections.

Steps

Step 1: Your first step is to melt the beeswax on low heat; you need to keep stirring it continuously. There is no requirement to purchase a thermometer in case you can keep the heat at a lower level and permit the wax to gradually melt. After all, the basic aim is to keep this project as simple as possible. In this project, I use only half a pound of wax. Ten votives can be made out of a pound of beeswax. You should ensure that stirring should be done continuously. You should not let it simmer or burn.

Step 2: Flutter dyes are being used to color the beeswax in order to make things easier. These dyes look cute and it is an extremely hassle-free and easy way of coloring your votive candles. You can get a medium shade when you use one flutter dye for every pound. You will see a darker shade upon using two flutter dyes. Using half will give it a pastel shade. It is fun to do these little experiments and see the results.

Step 3: After your beeswax has almost fully melted, your next step should be to add the flutter dye. How much you want to add is entirely up to you. The measurement I use is half flutter dye for half the pound of your beeswax. Keep stirring until the remaining wax and dye have melted completely.

Step 4: Now remove the wax from the heat and pour your scent. Make sure you keep stirring. It is all right to use a maximum of 1.5 ounces of fragrance to one pound of beeswax. The best way to mix is by using one pound to one ounce. It will be easy to remember and is simple to measure.

Step 5: Your molds should be made ready. The wick pins should be placed inside the votive molds on the surface, so that pouring the wax is easier for you. These wick pins will act as your wicks' place card holder. You can use some parchment paper so that the surface is protected from the spillover of rogue wax, if any.

Step 6: The fun part in your candle making process begins now. Pour the candle beeswax into each one of the molds. However, you need to do it instantly. The beeswax may start cooling down if your waiting period is too long. It may solidify inside the pouring pot. In case it comes to that, you need to melt it again. It is entirely up to you where and when you should stop pouring. There are some people, for instance, who love filling them until they begin to overflow.

Step 7: It is better to place your fully cooled votives for five to ten minutes inside the freezer, rather than messing with the chemicals released from the molds. The candle beeswax gets properly released from the mold due to the cold. The same holds true for any kind of candle holder. For example, if there are remains of burned candles in some containers, then you can place them in the freezer so that the beeswax can release magically.

Step 8: Next, you should tug your wick pin slightly so that your candle can be removed. Then you need to turn your candle upside down.

Step 9: Tap the wick pin on the countertop so that the wick pin gets released. Push down carefully, then the pin should be pulled out with caution.

Step 10: Next, press the base of the wick clip strongly into the beeswax to ensure that the wick remains in place. You should trim your candle wicks in accordance to your requirement. That is all you need to do.

Your homemade votive candles are ready. Don't they look rustic and simply gorgeous? You will be definitely super thrilled now to start your DIY project on these candles. You can use flutter dyes such as blue, light blue, lavender and peach.

Chapter VI: Common Mistakes to Avoid While Making Candles at Home

Weak flame from the candle

Weak flame is one of the most common problems that candle users face. Candles which burn with weak flames not only do not give out enough light, but they are at the risk of extinguishing themselves at any moment. Candle makers need to take utmost care in order to prevent this problem. There are two common reasons for a candle burning with a weak flame. First, the wick used for the candle is way too small; the other reason is the wax used.

The wick is a key component of the candle. The wick works as the fuel-supplying mechanism to the flame of the candle. Most of the contemporary wicks are fabricated by stiffly knitting cotton or other fabric threads; many of them even have a core inside them. There are no dearths of wicks in the market. Candle makers need to do their research thoroughly and choose the right wick for the particular candle they are making. It is even advisable to experiment with different types of wick to come to the final conclusion.

Wick size needs to be appropriate for the candle flame to be just the right size. The right sized wick ensures that the pool of melted wax is sufficient enough to support optimal burning time. If the wick is too large, then the candle will not last long. As a result, the wax is not being burnt efficiently. If the wick is too small, it will result in a deep pool of melted wax. This makes the flame weak and more likely to be extinguished by itself before it is completely utilized. The only way to determine the best wick for different candles is by testing the burn characteristics with different wicks for each candle.

Again, the best way to determine the ideal wick for the candles you are making is by experimenting with the various kinds of wicks and their varying sizes. Although testing might seem cumbersome, it is the only way one can get better at candle making. Experimenting with different types of wicks and candles makes one good at designing their own unique candles.

Sometimes a candle burns with a weak flame because the wax is not matched with the right wick. For the candle to burn with a decent sized flame, it needs to have a consistent supply of melted wax. Tougher waxes which do not melt at the proper rate cannot provide melted wax consistently for the wick to consume. Candle makers can prevent this by using the right wax for the right wicks, or by using lesser amount of hardening agent when making the candles.

A little care in the above two aspects will ensure that your candles do not suffer from the problem of burning with a weak flame.

Candle tunneling

The perfect candle burns utilizing each and every drop of wax efficiently. Candle tunneling is a phenomenon, wherein the flame consumes wax only from the central portion of the candle closer to the wick. This excludes the wax at the edges of the candle. Most amateur candle makers have mistaken that certain candles normally burn like this, but nothing can be farther from the truth. It can be hard to relight candles for later use if candles are allowed to tunnel continuously. Tunneling can even lead to loss of wick altogether.

The only reason that any candle suffers from the problem of tunneling is because the wick is too small for the candle. So, candle makers need to take extra care to ensure that the wick is of just the right size to support a proper sized flame. A proper sized flame is one, which melts wax throughout the edge of the candle and not just near the wick.

Another solution to prevent tunneling of candles is by using softer wax to make candles. Softer wax will ensure that the wax will melt easily; thus, it eliminates the chances of tunneling. This is the reason the wick needs to be properly matched to both the candle size and the kind of wax used. In case a hardening agent is being used for making the candles, the quantity of the hardening agent used can be varied to make the wax softer than usual to prevent the tunneling. The best way to determine the perfect wick and wax for a particular kind of candle is by experimenting with different wicks and different waxes. There are no shortcuts to design the perfect candle.

What to do when your candle has a poor fragrance?

A lot of candle makers face this problem whenever they try to invent newer kinds of scented candles. The thing is: this problem can be caused by a number of reasons. Hence, it is a bit difficult to pinpoint the exact reason for the candle giving out poor fragrance. In this section we shall discuss what you can do as a candle maker to prevent this problem from ever occurring.

Incompatible wax: It does not matter how powerful or premium the fragrance oils are; sometimes they just do not blend well with the wax used. This is especially true for beeswax. Before choosing a fragrance oil, it is imperative that people see how compatible it is with the wax of which they are making the candles.

Insufficient quantity of fragrance oil: Candle makers often utilize less fragrance oil since it comes in the concentrated form. Ideally, most fragrance oils should be blended at the rate of one ounce per pound of wax for optimum fragrance. However, these measurements may vary with different brands of fragrance oils, so this fact needs to be verified before using them for candles. Excessive fragrance oil usage can also turn problematic; it interferes with steady flame of the candle.

Incompatible temperature mixing: The fragrance oil should blend completely with the melted wax to be effective. Fragrance oil should be blended to the melted wax, only when it is in the temperature range of 180° to 185° Fahrenheit. Introducing the fragrance oil at a higher temperature will cause it to burn out, whereas introducing it at a lower temperature will most likely result in cold throw. The melted wax starts to cool down as soon as it is taken away from the heat source. Furthermore, adding fragrance oil will also lead to cooling of the melted wax. So, take care to pour the fragrance oil at the right temperature range for best results.

Does your candle smoke as it burns?

It is natural for smoke to emanate when a substance is burned. Typically, excessive smoke is produced when there is insufficient amount of oxygen available for burning. By taking some precautions while making the candles, you can easily ensure that your candles burn brightly without giving smoke out.

Excessive fragrance oil: Fragrance oil should only be used in limited quantities. Most people think that, increasing the amount of fragrance oil in the candles makes it give out stronger fragrance. However, this causes the candles to smoke while they are burning. Furthermore, it can even lead to leakage of fragrance oil, which can result in dangerous fire hazards.

Improper wick size: One cannot simply choose any random wick without doing any research. The thickness of the candle is a key parameter, which determines the characteristics of the wick that needs to be used. The wicks should always be trimmed to one fourth of an inch, in order for it to burn efficiently.

Coloring additives: Most amateur candle makers use pigments instead of candle dyes to color their candles. This is the most common reason for candles to smoke while they burn. It is imperative that only candle dyes are used whenever the wax out of the candles is going to be colored. Furthermore, the candle dyes themselves must be used in moderation, or else excessive candle dyes can also lead to smoking candles.

Not giving attention to the temperatures: Maintaining the right temperatures at the different stages of candle making is extremely important. Waxes may have different temperatures specified for different stages like melting, fragrance oil blending and pouring. Candle makers need to ensure that the waxes are in the right temperature to that process for which they are subjected.

What to do when the candle does not come out of the molds?

Most people are unaware that the candles contract when they cool down. Removing them from the mold should be pretty easy because they shrink upon cooling. It is important you know that one should never try to cut the wax to remove the candle from the mold. In this section, we shall first see how to prevent this problem from occurring. Then, we shall see how to solve this problem when it occurs.

Candles get stuck to the molds because of the damages the molds have. Imperfections like interior scratches, depressions or damages will render the mold unusable for candle making.

Some candle makers make it a point to apply lube to the mold prior to pouring the hot wax in them. This serves as a countermeasure to prevent the candles sticking to the molds.

Lastly, we shall see what to do, when the candle is already stuck inside the mold.

1. It is imperative that the candle has completely cooled down before it can be removed from the mold. Trying to remove the candle from the mold when it is still warm damages the candle.

2. In case the candle is not removable from the mold after cooling down, it should be kept in the refrigerator till it becomes cold to touch. Once it is really cold, it should come out from the mold easily once it is really cold.

3. If in spite of cooling in the fridge and the candle is still not removable from the mold, then it should be kept in the freezer for some time. Ideally, the candle should come out of the mold without much effort. If it still does not come out, this step needs to be repeated about three to four times with longer durations of freezing till it becomes removable.

How to avoid cracks in your candles?

One of the most common problems which almost all the candle makers have faced is cracking. However, it can be avoided altogether if one takes some precautions.

Perfect candles are those which have all its constituents properly matched to one another. Each and every component of the candle, right from the wax up to the wick, needs to be carefully matched with one another. Another key requirement for making the perfect candles is the temperature. Everything from the pouring temperature to the temperature at which the candles are kept, all play a major part in determining how well the candle burns. We shall see some precautions to prevent candle cracking.

1. The melted wax should cool slowly without receiving any external help to cool down. The molds which will receive the melted wax needs to be at the room temperature in order to prevent quick cooling of the wax. The workspace where candles are made should not have areas of uneven temperatures to ensure that the candles do not form cracks.

2. When one is making candles during the winter months, care should be taken to increase the temperature at which the melted wax is poured into the mold. It is advisable to always use a thermometer when pouring melted wax.

3. Seasonal variations in pouring temperatures can be avoided if one makes candles in a temperature-controlled room at all times.

4. In order to smoothen out the surface of the candles, one can make use of heat guns as needed.

5. The candles should always be kept in tepid places away from direct sunlight.

Although the above measures are effective to prevent cracks in candles in most cases, there might be other reasons for cracks emerging in candles. In such cases, the cause needs to be independently determined to solve the issue.

Does your finished candle show signs of bubbles and pitting?

Candles form minuscule bubbles and pits for quite a lot of reasons. The best thing that a candle maker can do to prevent this problem is to pour the molten wax at a higher temperature in the range recommended by the wax supplier. Ensuring that the mold is preheated can also help in mitigating this problem. Simple things like allowing the candles to cool naturally away from drafts can solve problems like these.

Pouring the molten wax at the right temperature is absolutely essential for making immaculate candles. If the wax is poured when it is cooler, than it needs to be while pouring, the air bubbles formed do not get a chance to escape as the wax sets a lot quicker than it should.

Some candle makers utilize water baths after pouring the molten wax to ensure that the candles have smooth surfaces. For this to work, the mold needs to be removed from the water bath as soon as it is filled. Then it should be allowed to cool naturally at room temperature.

Candle makers should take care to ensure that no water gets into any of the ingredients of the candles, such as wax or fragrance oil. Even a little amount of water can result in pits and bubbles in the candles, no matter how careful the candle maker is in all the other aspects.

Using excessive mold releases for candles is also another common cause for candles to develop pits. Most expert candle makers, recommend using only silicone-based mold release. Even this mold release has to be used mildly.

Dirty molds are another common reason for candles to develop pits. It is imperative that candle makers take special care to ensure that the molds are clean before they pour melted wax into it.